The Mystery of Being

Books of Gabriel Marcel from St. Augustine's Press

The Mystery of Being: vol. I: *Reflection and Mystery*

The Mystery of Being: vol. II: *Faith and Reality*

Man against Mass Society

Homo Viator: Introduction to the Metaphysic of Hope

Thou Shall Not Die (selected and arranged by Anne Marcel)

A Gabriel Marcel Reader (edited by Brendan Sweetman)

The Mystery of Being
II: Faith and Reality

Gabriel Marcel

Translated by G. S. Fraser

ST. AUGUSTINE'S PRESS
South Bend, Indiana
2001

Library of Congress Cataloging in Publication Data
Marcel, Gabriel, 1889–1973.
  [Mystére de l'être. English]
  The mystery of being / Gabriel Marcel ; translated by G.S. Fraser.
    p.   cm.
  Originally published: London : Harvill Press, 1950–1951. (Gifford lectures; 1949–1950)
  Contents: v. 1. Reflection and mystery – v. 2. Faith and reality.
  ISBN 1-890318-85-X (v. 1: alk. paper) – ISBN 1-890318-86-8 (v. 2: alk. paper)
  1. Ontology. 2. Faith. 3. Reality. I. Title. II. Series:Gifford lectures ; 1949–1950.
B2430.M253M83 2000
110 – dc21   00-062619

∞ *The paper used in this publication meets the minimum requirements of the American National Standard for Information Sciences – Permanence of Paper for Printed Materials, ANSI Z39.48-1984.*

St. Augustine's Press acknowledges the kind courtesy of Regnery Publishing, Inc., and its president, Alfred S. Regnery, for granting translation rights to this volume.

ST. AUGUSTINE'S PRESS
www.staugustine.net

CONTENTS

v

be interpreted as an *appeal*: there is a demand for, there would be a demand for, the existence of being.

It is an exigence for *fulness*: that is to say that being cannot be divorced from value: which does not mean that it can be identified with *perfection* (criticism of the *ens realissimum*).

IV. THE LEGITIMACY OF ONTOLOGY ..

Under what conditions can being be substantified?

1. Is it legitimate for particular beings and not for being in itself?
2. Is it illegitimate in both cases: Is it legitimate only for being in itself?
3. In both cases should we respect the use which is made of the substantive in speech?

If particular beings are de-substantified, that amounts to functionalizing them: the first hypothesis, then, must be accepted, provided that we do not look on beings as units, but as centres, focus-points of which the wholes do not form *groups* but rather *constellations*.

But can it be thought that *beings* exist in a universe which is such that it would nevertheless be possible to say: being does not exist? If there is no being, no more can there be individual beings. Thought is accordingly doomed to waver between two interpretations which are only nominally distinct; nevertheless it can go beyond them (secondary reflection) by showing that the enquiry into being does not refer to the objectivity of a massive whole of beings which one might call Being in itself, and that it is inseparable from the exigence of being.

V. OPINION AND FAITH ....

Distinction between opinion—conviction—faith.

1. There is no opinion except about what one does not know; but this lack of knowledge does not make itself apparent, and it wavers between impression and affirmation, between *seeming so* and *claiming that*. It is a seeming which tends, thanks to lack of reflection, to turn into a claim.

   In this sense, the atheist *has* opinions: 'for my part, I claim that God does not exist'; 'if God existed, he would not allow . . . etc.'

2. Conviction appears as an unshakable position, definitive, without the power to justify these characteristics.

3. Faith: movement from the closed (opinion: conviction) to the open. To believe is not to believe *that*, but to believe *in*, that is, to open a credit in the favour of, to place oneself at the disposal of . . .

Through faith, I take on a fundamental engagement which turns upon what I *am*, and I open myself to a personal or supra-personal reality.

VI. PRAYER AND HUMILITY .... page 85

THE PRAYING CONSCIOUSNESS

Faith, which opens me to an authentic and transcendent reality, implies humility and prayer.

Humility is not the same as the fact of self-humiliation: it is not a quality, but a mode of being which includes the recognition of the nothingness of the creature and the affirmation of the sacred. Prayer can be more pure or less pure: the self-centred request is impure; pure prayer cannot be conceived as remaining unanswered; it transcends the hypothesis, 'There is someone who is listening to me' or, 'There is no one'; it is a way of uniting oneself with . . . i.e., the true spirit of prayer recognizes intersubjectivity.

VII. FREEDOM AND GRACE .... page 108

Within what limits can I assert myself as a free being? To be free is not to do what I want: real will is distinct from desire.

Nor is it the making of an arbitrary choice: the 'liberté d'indifférence' presupposes the insignificance of the stake, and there is no freedom if the stake has no real importance. Freedom, then, is not something that I note, but something about which I make a decision from which there is no appeal. The free act is the significant act which contributes to making me what I am. By freedom I am given back to myself: that is to say that freedom does not stand on its own feet, it presupposes this concession, this gift, this grace with which it is mysteriously dovetailed.

VIII. TESTIMONY .... page 125

The inter-relation of freedom and grace lies beyond the verifiable: but is there still reality beyond the verifiable?

The reflection which asks this question dissociates itself from the praying 'ego'. There can be synthesis between both in the Hegelian sense, but there may be some sort of harmony. The believer must indulge in reflection as the trial which will enable him to purify his faith, i.e., to progress from a certainty which he is always tempted to look on as a possession, to a certainty that *he is* a *testimony*.

Through testimony, we go beyond the question which is put by reflection. There is no exteriority of the witness in relation to that to which he bears witness; testimony does not *bear on* a fact or an event which is simply stated; it transcends at once both the objective and the subjective; it is in this sense that it may be called creative (creative testimony).

IX. DEATH AND HOPE

The real trial is that by which the believer is called upon to go beyond *evil*: connection between evil and death, which shows that immortality is the stake of a decisive metaphysical choice.

How can we use '*choice*' in this connection? Is it not rather a question of an objective enquiry whose end is to distinguish between the *fact* and the *imaginary*?

In reality, immortality cannot be thought of as the immortality of a thing or a simple *image*: it is that of a *bond*; that is why it is beyond the reach of curiosity or demonstration. Only hope, a prophetic assurance that the intersubjective destiny is called upon to continue its development, a reaction against a state of captivity, is consistent with it.

X. CONCLUSION

Modern man is in an eschatological position. That is true quite independently of any scriptural reference to an Apocalypse. It is in relation to this situation that the indissoluble unity of faith, hope and charity should be stated, such as it is seen to be in the light of a philosophy of intersubjectivity; this latter widens out into a polyphonic conception of the Universal, in the name of which the spirit of excommunication which animates all false theologies should be condemned. The proofs of the existence of God should not be looked on as demonstrative proofs—though that does not imply that they are entirely without value. But this value depends on a certain spiritual condition which is less and less ours. In the religious perspective, this may seem paradoxical ; but the paradox must not be taken in an irrationalist sense. The purer faith is, the closer it comes to the spirit of truth, as the light of salvation. Salvation is nothing, if it is not liberation from death: this liberation could take place only on a supra-terrestrial plane and in dimensions which are not those of history. The Hegelian idea of history, which is the source of the vilest idolatries of our time, is only a counterfeit or a perversion of a much more profound thought, a thought which cannot be embodied without the help of myth—the price we have to pay for our own condition which is that of incarnate beings. Here it is that philosophy reaches its boundaries, and awaits the first glimmers of the fires of revelation.

FAITH AND REALITY

CHAPTER I

THE QUESTION OF BEING

AS I stand on the threshold of this second series, I have the same feeling of giddiness as that which comes over a traveller when he reaches the edge of an abyss into which he must take a headlong plunge. Last year we were crossing what was certainly broken country; there were traps of which we had to beware, but we escaped any precipitous fall. What, then, is this abyss into which we shall have to fling ourselves?

It is this: this time we shall have to ask ourselves questions about the nature of being as such. As soon as we do that, it will be as though we had to move in a new dimension. But I must add a warning. It is only too clear that this new dimension will have to conform with those in which our earlier enquiries were contained. I shall make use of the method which I often found useful last year of continually reviving the metaphors with which I reinforce my arguments. I shall say that everything happens now, rather as in a fugue when a new voice intervenes. It would not be enough to say that the new voice is added to the earlier ones: in some way it changes the whole colour of the complete work. Later, it should be necessary for us—and this, I grant, is rather an awkward task— to keep the spatial metaphor present in our minds simultaneously with the musical metaphor. Thus we shall gain a more distinct idea of the sort of transformation, of the sort of revival, which this second series of lectures must attempt to introduce.

Now, even more than before, we shall have to be continually on our guard against the traps that are hidden in language; and since it is without doubt much more difficult in the domain of strict metaphysics to advance by means of examples and concrete illustrations, I promise you, and I promise myself, that in making so far as possible concrete and even in a way dramatic transpositions, I shall push to the extreme limit the caution that I exercised in the first series. In this matter I find my position a little puzzling, and I do not think it would be a waste of time to try to make it more precise.

After more than thirty years, I have been going through the unpublished notes of my first metaphysical enquiries, and I am rather astonished to find that the problems which engaged me then are precisely those which seem to me today to be the most important; I should even say that they are the only ones, when you come to analyse them finally, which are worthy of holding the attention of a philosopher. All the rest can ultimately be dismissed as chatter. I should go even further— the solutions (presuming that 'solution' is the right word to use) which I was then—i.e. before the first world war—outlining, do not differ fundamentally from those I shall put forward today. Nevertheless, life has intervened since that distant time, with all the joys and sorrows, all the discoveries and frustrations that it can bring to any being. I find since that time that the formulae which used to give me a certain amount of satisfaction, are no longer apposite ; they were much too abstract. I purposely say a 'certain amount of satisfaction' because even in those days I felt in my heart an invincible distrust of pure abstraction; and, as I have often said since, I made use, in a way, of dialectic in order to get rid of dialectic.

Remembering this, and to continue with a musical comparison—I shall more than once make use of such—I should be tempted to say that my thought has not undergone *evolution* in the sense which is generally given to that word, but rather that it has moved by working gradually and progressively at the orchestration of a number of themes which were the initial data. This word *data* itself raises some obscure and perhaps insoluble problems. We should be certainly under a delusion if we imagined that on the one hand we have a thought whose make-up is fixed once and for all, and on the other hand themes and motifs supplied to it from outside. We cannot make such a picture for ourselves without forgetting precisely the thing we are discussing. The true picture is rather that thought—and I understand by that not thought in general, but a concrete, personalized, thought—takes shape only in so far as it discovers the exigencies by which it will be qualified. You will remember last year I made frequent, perhaps almost too frequent, use of this word *exigence*. Neither the word 'need' nor the word 'requirement' conveys the meaning of this word, which corresponds to the German *Forderung*. We shall meet it again now; and while we had then to be satisfied with speaking of the exigence of transcendence, we shall now be led to examine the exigence of God. We could say, I believe, in future that the exigence of God is simply the exigence of transcendence disclosing its true face, a face that was shown to us before shrouded in veils. I said at the beginning of this lecture that we should have to move in the dimension of being. Now I must add that we shall deal with the exigence of God, and, a still deeper matter, with faith in God. We shall have to ask ourselves under what conditions, short of a revelation properly so called, it is possible for us to make any affirmations about what God is, or at least about what He is not

3

or cannot be. But we shall have to make a very close examination—and this I consider will be one of the essential objects of our enquiry—of the way in which strictly metaphysical enquiry, which concerns what I have called *being as such*, is related to religious philosophy: or rather we must find out how the two are interlocked. Although many of the most famous metaphysicians of the past seem to give us direct encouragement, we cannot lay it down as a principle and a starting point that *being as such* (if it can be thought of, which is not *a priori* certain) is necessarily to be identified with that to which a believing consciousness gives the name of God. Let us accordingly lay it down once for all, as emphatically as we can, that it is only the living witness, that is to say the believing consciousness, which can decide what can or cannot be regarded as God. I shall lay it down as a principle—and this postulate will doubtless become clarified later—that it is beyond the power of any philosophy (we can leave theology out of it for the moment) to force a *coup d'état* which instals as God something which the believing consciousness refuses to recognize as such. It will be necessary, no doubt, to go more fully into what we mean by the believing consciousness, and in order to do this we shall have to make use of some of the conclusions to which our last year's enquiries led us.

Nevertheless, the approach to this sanctuary of traditional ontology is bound to overpower us with a feeling of fatigue and oppression, I should even say, unhappily, of boredom. Is it to be part of our duty to dig into the depths of Aristotelian metaphysics; worse still, into the teaching of the schoolmen who continued Aristotle's work? I shall make no bones about it—I have no such intention. If I had, there would be a danger that this second series of lectures would come down to being

4

nothing but a misleading resumé of the history of philosophy: and, whether it be misleading or not, there is no University Professor in this country or any other who would not, after all, be better qualified than I am to give such a resumé. At the risk of appearing rather rash or cavalier in my treatment, I propose to assume that all the essential historical background is familiar, and to come straight to the question, What is Being? I shall ask myself how we can give to Being a meaning that is intelligible for us.

I say 'for us' with purpose. I shall not give a detailed repetition of what I have already said about the necessity of transcending the plane of thought in general, or better, as Heidegger would express it, of the *Man*; remembering that this is of course the German word *Man*, not *Mann*, or the French pronoun *on*. To put it in a more positive way, let us say that I have to think not only for myself, but for us; in other words for everyone who may have contact with the thought which is mine. There is a sense in which we are all historical beings; that is to say, that we come after other beings from whom we have received a great deal, and this precisely in a way which gives us something by which we are differentiated from them: but at the same time we come *before* other beings, and these will find that they have the same relation to us as we have to those who came before us. In every instance these relations are more complex than at first appears, and we should do violence to their nature if we tried to fit them into a serialized pattern. Thus it is that the thought of a philosopher who lived many years ago, Plato for example, can be revitalized as our road winds round, can be recharged with an efficacy which it did not seem to possess at certain earlier stages. In this sense, though it might seem paradoxical, it would not be too much to say that something like an exchange takes place between the present and the distant past. Moreover, this is only an illustration of the important idea, to which we shall often have occasion to return, that in the order of the spiritual the distinction between the close and the distant changes its nature and tends to transcend itself.

The question arises, however, whether, when we insist on the 'fact that each one of us must be a philosopher both *hic et nunc* and for those who may later have to cross his path, we do not run the risk of overlooking the essential fact that to be a philosopher is after all to think *sub specie aeterni*. But we must here point out a possible source of grave misunderstanding. That phrase is, in truth, ambiguous: it may mean that we intend to abstract from the experience which is necessarily peculiar to ourselves, to transport ourselves into a sort of mental stratosphere; or it can have an entirely different meaning. We shall have good reason to ask whether the notion that we can find an escape by climbing into such a region immune from change, is not after all an illusion. In the final balance it is neither proved nor even demonstrable that I can abstract from my own experience, except of course in so far as I propose to confine myself to the study of certain abstract elements of reality — or rather, let us say, of certain structural conditions of the type of knowledge which is ours. But to philosophize *sub specie aeterni* may mean something very different from just wiping the slate clean. It may mean devoting myself to understanding my own life as fully as possible; and where I use the word 'life' in that connection, I could equally well use the word 'experience'. If I try to do so, I shall most likely be led to a strange and wonderful discovery—that the more I raise myself to a really concrete perception of my own experience, the more, by that very act, shall I be attuned to an effective understanding of others, of the experience of others. Nothing indeed can be more important and helpful than to realize this fully.

But here, as before, I shall need to refer to the experience of the specific type of creation, which is that of the dramatist. The virtue proper to dramatic creation, where the creation is authentic, consists in the exorcizing of the ego-centric spirit. But one may perhaps ask whether ego-centric is not precisely what concrete understanding of self always is? I shall categorically deny that. Ego-centrism, on the contrary, is possible only in a being which has not properly mastered its own experience, which has not really assimilated it. It is worth devoting our attention to this for a few moments, for it has an important bearing on the rest of our enquiry.

In so far as I am obsessed by an ego-centric preoccupation, that preoccupation acts as a barrier between me and others; and by others must be understood in this connection the life and the experience of others. But let us suppose this barrier has been overthrown. The paradox is that at the same time it is also my own personal experience that I rediscover in some way, for in reality my experience is in a real communciation with other experiences. I cannot be cut off from the one without being cut off from the other. In other words, ego-centrism is always a cause of blindness: but there is no blindness that can be localized. I mean that you cannot be utterly blind to one thing without being blind to other things as well. All this may seem odd at first glance, but it is nevertheless evident to me that while this seems at first an *a priori* view, yet experience adds confirmation to it. It is because the egoist confines his thought to himself that he is fundamentally in the dark about himself. He does not know his real needs, he does not realize that he betrays himself just to the extent to which he concentrates all his attention upon himself.

But the corollary is equally true, and it is precisely this corollary which is of importance to us for the next steps in our enquiry. A complete and concrete knowledge of oneself cannot be heauto-centric; however paradoxical it may seem, I should prefer to say that it must be hetero-centric. The fact is that we can understand ourselves by starting from the other, or from others, and only by starting from them; and one could even anticipate what we shall have to recognize much later, and add that it is only in this perspective that a legitimate love of self can be conceived. Fundamentally, I have no reason to set any particular store by myself, except in so far as I know that I am loved by other beings who are loved by me. Love of self can have a true foundation only by using others as a medium, and that medium is our only safeguard against ego-centrism and our only assurance that it will have the character of lucidity which otherwise it inevitably loses.

It may appear at first that these remarks have no bearing upon our original enquiry. How can they nevertheless serve to advance it?

Two things seem to me to be of importance. First, we must understand that this enquiry can be developed only if we take a certain fullness of life as our starting point; secondly, we must at the same time note well that this fullness of life can in no circumstances be that of my own personal experience considered in an exclusively private aspect, considered in as much as it is *just mine*; rather must it be that of a whole which is implied by the relation to the *with*, by the *togetherness*, on which last year I laid such emphasis. The intersubjectivity at

8

which we so painfully arrived must be, in fact, the ground upon which we must base ourselves for our further enquiries this year.

But to take up such a position immediately throws into relief the essentially anti-cartesian character of the metaphysic to which we shall have to direct ourselves. It is not enough to say that it is a metaphysic of being; it is a metaphysic of *we are* as opposed to a metaphysic of *I think*. It is most instructive to note in our own days that Sartre, who makes use of a cartesianism which in other ways he has mutilated (since he has deprived it of the theology which crowns it) is himself obliged to take the other only as a threat to my liberty; or, strictly speaking, as a possible source of seduction which it is very difficult not to interpret in a sadistic or masochistic sense. When the author of *Huis-Clos* writes 'Hell—that's other people', he supplies his own evidence of his impossible position; whether it is for reasons which belong to existential psychoanalysis or whether it is simply because of his meta-physical postulates, he can have no understanding of *philia* or *agape*. In the end it is only on the one hand the domain of *eros*, with its formidable ambiguity, so far as it coincides with want or desire, which is accessible to him, or, on the other hand, that of a community of work which creates teams united by the knowledge of a task which has to be done; and it is only if you look at it from outside that you can see in this a genuine sort of solidarity. It must necessarily be so. It could be otherwise only if he repudiated, explicitly or implicitly, the principles of his ontology: the fundamental opposition between being-in-itself and being-for-itself which by definition makes impossible intersubjectivity in the precise sense I have given to the word, or, if you wish, makes it impossible to be

9

open to the other, to welcome him in the deepest sense of the word, and to become at the same time more accessible to oneself.

But it may be asked whether the inter-subjectivity upon which I seek to ground my ontology can lead to some simple proposition that can be clearly expressed. Is there anything in it which could be put into the form of a logical principle? Or is it not rather a simple inexpressible intuition which runs, after all, the risk of being reduced to just a sentimental disposition? If it is not an affirmation which can be expressed in words, is it not simply a wish which mistakes itself for an assertion?

But this word *assertion* should hold our attention for a few moments. What can I *assert*? A fact, and nothing but a fact, since the fact is the only thing which is presented to me. But it is apparent by definition that what I may call the inter-subjective nexus cannot be given to me, since I am myself in some way involved in it. It may not perhaps be inaccurate to say that this nexus is in fact the necessary condition for anything being given to me—at least if 'given' is taken in its narrowest meaning: and if this might seem arguable, one should at least recognize that it is only this nexus which can allow the thing which is given to 'speak to me'.

Now, if I am to answer it, it must in some sort of way speak to me. Thus we can see the position we must necessarily take up towards the embarrassing questions which presented themselves to us just now. Without doubt the intersubjective nexus cannot be in any way asserted: it can only be acknowledged. Here again we meet an idea which has already taken up much of our attention. This recognition must assuredly be patient of translation into an expressible affirmation. At the same time we should be careful to remember that the affirmation should possess a special character, that of being the root of every expressible affirmation. I should readily agree that it is the mysterious root of language. These words should be taken literally; and you will understand that I am here referring to the definition of mystery which I put forward in my first volume. But this point is so important and at the same time, I must admit, presents such difficulties, that it is well to labour it as we continue to circle round the elusive centre of the problem.

At first it certainly seems that there is a difference only of perspective between what I now call the intersubjective nexus and that to which last year I gave, when speaking of truth, the name of intelligible milieu; one might say that the intelligible milieu or medium is only the projection on an ideal plane of what existentially speaking presents itself to us as the intersubjective nexus. This elucidation is, however, quite insufficient. I have had the misfortune to note by my own experience that when we adhere to this expression of intersubjective nexus, what I am tempted to call a mental clot is formed, which interrupts the circulation of thought; and it is precisely this circulation of thought which we have to re-establish. I mean that the words, so to say, interpose themselves between me and the thought I am driving at; they get a bogey-like and unwelcome reality of their own; they become an obstacle instead of remaining an instrument. What exactly are we looking for? We have agreed that it is not a fact, but no more is it a form in the traditional meaning of the word. It would be better to speak of a structure, so long as we remember that when we speak of a structure, we commonly call up the idea of an object which is patient of being observed from the outside. But here the point with which we are concerned is what I should make bold to call the *inside of a structure,* of an inside, moreover, to which we must realize we are entirely unable, in our condition of finite beings and in as much as we are tied to an earthly dwelling, to imagine, to set virtually before ourselves, a corresponding outside. This should help to throw some light on the strange and highly disconcerting character of the foundations on which we have to build as best we can the rudiments of a metaphysic; and we should doubtless emphasize this even more, so that we may throw as much light as possible on those foundations. The great difficulty with which we are now faced comes from the fact that our thinking has had to bear the weight of idealist teachings. It has great trouble in freeing itself from them and can normally address itself to any object only by concentrating upon *I think,* or upon something which is simply a vaguer modification of *I think*—*I feel,* for example, or *I see.* But here we are called upon for an entirely different type of effort. We may say that we have to place ourselves on this side of the insularity of the ego; we must get to the centre of the actual element from which the island emerges and presents itself to our view. What, then, is the element of which I was able to say that it was the inside of a structure? In the first place, can we here legitimately ask the question, 'What is it'? We must first make a preliminary analysis.

If, for example, I am going for a walk and I find a flower which I have never seen before, and if I ask, 'What is this flower?', that question has a relatively precise meaning. Perhaps my companion can tell me the name of the flower, and I may then consider the matter settled. But perhaps it will not be enough for me to know the name which is commonly given to it; and if I have some idea of botany, I may ask to what family the flower belongs. If I am told that it is an orchis, I shall conclude that it presents certain characteristics in common with other flowers which I have already seen and which I am able to recognize. There is thus a possibility of progress in the answering of the question, 'What is this flower?' Nevertheless we see directly that even the more scientific answer, which enables me to classify the flower, is not an exhaustive answer; in fact in a certain sense it is no answer at all; it is even an evasion. By that I mean that it disregards the singularity of this particular flower. What has actually happened is as though my question had been interpreted as follows—'to what thing other than itself, can this flower itself be reduced?' But now we find the real paradox—the first unscientific answer, which consisted in giving the name of the flower, although it had practically no rational basis, yet satisfied the demand in me which the interpretation by reduction tends on the contrary to frustrate. It is true that the satisfaction which is here given by the name seems as though it could be felt only by a consciousness which has been arrested at a pre-scientific stage, practically at an infantile stage where the name is taken as being one body with the thing named and so usurps a magical potency. We shall have to come back later, perhaps, to this important point.

In all these instances it is important to note, though it has often been insufficiently appreciated, that the question 'What is it?' always has reference to something that can be given a distinctive designation; to look at it more profoundly, it has reference in every instance to an order that implies threefold inter-relations. To go back to the elementary example I made use of before, I point out the flower—this flower—to my companion; he has more botanical knowledge than I have, and

I count on him to explain to me what it is. It is, of course, understood that I could look it up in a book of botany, which would serve the same purpose; or even, supposing that I am alone, that I could consult my own knowledge. In all these instances, there are the three elements, the three terms subsist. Might one not, indeed, ask whether fundamentally the question, if it is taken in its simplest form, will not be found to rest on a plane which is not threefold but twofold, as though I had asked the flower 'Who are you?' But to put the question in that form is inevitably to distort it. It is not the flower which tells me its name through the medium of the botanist; I shall be forced to see that the name is a convention, it has been agreed to give that particular name to the flower in which I am interested. By that convention we slip out of the realm of being properly so called, and all that we shall learn will be what one can say about the flower if we leave out the one important thing—the singularity which forced my attention, or which, in other words, spoke to me.

We have now reached some conclusions which may turn out to be important for subsequent enquiries. We must be careful to remember the starting point of the analysis we have just made. We were asking ourselves what was the inter-subjective element from which the *ego* seems to emerge like an island rising from the waves. There is one point here, however, which deserves our close attention. I have been speaking as though this element could be pointed out or designated, in the sense in which I can point out the sea to someone else when I have seen it for the first time. In such a case I should not be satisfied with the answer, 'What you are looking at is the sea'; I could be given straightway a number of ideas about the sea, about its relation to the continent, to the whole surface of the earth, and so forth. But the element with which we are here concerned cannot really be designated; I should say, to put it briefly, that it cannot be contained in the designation of the 'this' or the 'that'; it is not, in fact, *either this or that.* It transcends any disjunction of this kind. It would not be inaccurate to say that it is an implied understanding which remains an implied understanding even when I try to focus my thought upon it. I agree that I shall almost inevitably be led to try to make a picture for myself of this element of inter-subjectivity; for example, I may conceive it as what I might call a fluid medium; but by that very act I shall deprive it of its own peculiar quality, which is a spiritual quality; I shall rob it of the character which enabled me to qualify it as inter-subjective. The best assurance against these misunderstandings is to have recourse to metaphors. These metaphors are more than mere metaphors, they are borrowed from the realm of reality, but of a non-optic, a non-spectacular, reality. I am now thinking primarily of the world in which I move when I am improvising on the piano, a world which is also, I am quite certain, the world in which the creative musician constructs his melodies. It is a world in which everything is in communication, in which everything is bound together. But we must remember that the fruit of our earlier discussion has been to pass beyond the plane of pure relations. What we commonly mean by that word is after all only an abstract reckoning up of what in this context should be recognized as living communication. The content of the words 'living communication', is still somewhat indistinct. I hope, though I cannot be sure of it, that in the course of our enquiry we may be able to elucidate it without unduly intellectualizing it.

I am afraid this first lecture has been somewhat disconcerting; but before I finish it I should like to try to answer a question which we cannot help asking ourselves as we reach the end of its tortuous progress. Can we admit that we have reached a point where we may identify being with intersubjectivity? Can we say that being *is* intersubjectivity?

I must answer immediately that it seems to me impossible to agree to his proposition if it is taken literally. The true answer, it seems to me, is something much more subtle, and needs an expression that is at once stricter and more intricate.

In these matters it is as well not to take too dogmatic a tone, but I think that one thing emerges: a thought which directs itself towards being, by that very act recreates around itself the intersubjective presence which a philosophy of monadist inspiration begins by expelling in the most arbitrary and high-handed manner. Remember, too, that the monadist philosopher's universe is such that it is difficult to imagine how the monadist philosophy itself could have taken root in it. Does it not presuppose a sort of inter-monad background, and does it not—at least when it is presented in its strictest form —at the same time expressly preclude the possibility of such a background? One might, perhaps, go further, and show that a consistent monadist thought is obliged to put too much emphasis on the domain of the *possible* at the expense of *being* taken in its mysterious positivity. These, however, are only preliminary considerations; at a later stage we should be able to clarify them. We could perhaps express it in language that can be grasped more immediately by saying that the more the *ego* attempts to assert for itself a central or autocratic position in the economy of consciousness, the more the density of being is attenuated. Conversely, the more the *ego* realizes that it is but one among others, among an infinity of others with which it maintains relations that are sometimes very difficult to trace, the more it tends to recapture the feeling of this density.

Nevertheless we must be on our guard; for if we were to confine ourselves to saying that the ego is simply *one* among others, we should reduce it to the status of one element in a numerical total. I have laid such stress upon intersubjectivity precisely because I wish to emphasize the presence of an underlying reality that is felt, of a community which is deeply rooted in ontology; without this human relations, in any real sense, would be unintelligible, or, to put it more accurately, would have to be looked upon as exclusively mythical.

This, then, is the conclusion we can draw at the end of this first lecture: whatever more precise characteristics may subsequently be assigned to an enquiry which bears upon being as such, we must recognize from the outset that the enquiry moves in a dimension which cannot be that of solipsist reflection, even in the most critical sense, that is to say of a reflection which is centred on the transcendental *Ego*, by whatever name we may call it. In more concrete language: *I concern myself with being only in so far as I have a more or less distinct consciousness of the underlying unity which ties me to other beings of whose reality I already have a preliminary notion.* In the light of the ideas which have not yet penetrated to the obscure regions in which we have tried to hack a path for ourselves, I should say of these beings that they are above all my fellow-travellers—my fellow-*creatures*—for once the English language can give us an expression for which there is no exact French equivalent; in French one would have had to paraphrase it, to extract the humble and at the same time inexhaustible depth of its meaning.

CHAPTER II

EXISTENCE AND BEING

I MUST now try to push deeper my examination of what is commonly called the ontological problem. From what I said last year it must, I think, be apparent that the problem is actually a mystery. But unfortunately there is a risk that the words 'ontological mystery' may degenerate into a pseudo-philosophical catch-phrase. We are again exposed to the danger that continually besets us, of seeing the significance of words and of thought itself weakened or corrupted, and it is only by a strenuous effort of reflection that we can escape this trying possibility.

It has often been remarked recently, and Etienne Gilson in particular has reminded us of it in his recent *L'Être et l'Essence** that the first difficulties we must take into account arise from our vocabulary itself. These difficulties are not quite the same in English as they are in French, but they are none the less grave.

In French the word *être* has the great inconvenience of having a double meaning; it is both a substantive and a verb. The philosophers whose inspiration derives from Heidegger's ontology have tried to avoid this ambiguity by introducing the word *étant*, used as a substantive, but it now seems very doubtful whether the word *étant* will gain currency among philosophers. Gilson indeed, notes that a seventeenth-century

* Paris, 1948

18

author, Scipion du Pleix, headed the second book of his metaphysic with the title '*Qu'est-ce que l'étant?*'; he adds that philosophers have made of the word *étant* a pure noun, using it simply and absolutely for anything at all, so long as it exists in truth, reality and fact, like: Angel, Man, Metal, Stone etc. In French, however, it is the word *être* which has been current even in this sense, and one could apparently conclude, according to Gilson, that it is the verbal sense which has prevailed in the end. Nevertheless the ambiguity remains; when I say in French, '*Qu'est-ce que l'être?*' do I simply wish to say, 'What does *to be* (i.e. the fact of being) mean?' or am I asking a very different question: do I by the word *être* really designate *l'étant*? If we use the Latin terms we say: does the enquiry bear upon *esse* or upon *ens*? We must realize that in English the ambiguity is even more embarrassing, as the word *being* corresponds exactly to *ens*, or to what I called in French *l'étant*. The difficulty then increases, unless we bring in another word such as *fact* or *act* to designate *esse* properly so called; and this springs from the purely grammatical fact that in English the present participle serves the same purpose as the infinitive used as a substantive does in Greek, for example, or in German.

I cannot help thinking that this ambiguity or amphibology is deep-rooted: we may even be tempted to believe that thought refuses more and more to face this enquiry; it is the most metaphysical of all enquiries, and it consists in asking ourselves what does *to be* mean, or again what is it that makes a being to be a *being*.

We can always, it is true, take refuge in the assumption that the reason why we spontaneously refuse to face this question is that it is indeed the most vain of all enquiries.

But what does *vain* mean in this particular context? Do we mean to say that it is useless in an entirely pragmatic sense? If so, it is clear that no philosopher could be held back by such a consideration. Must we dig deeper and say that there is a veto on such an enterprise, that it amounts to an attempt at trespassing in a domain which should remain inaccessible to a creature, in as much as it *is* a creature? When everything has been taken into account, I am not quite certain, indeed, that there is not some truth in that attitude. On the other hand, how could the philosopher resign himself to admitting that his road is blocked by a notice, *Vietato l'ingresso*? How could he deny himself the search for a clearer definition of *being* as *being*?

It is clear, in the first place, that this is not a question of an ordinary predicate, perhaps even not of a predicate at all: we may have to avail ourselves of the Aristotelian notion of transcendentals. It calls for only a most elementary philosophical reflection to realize that *to be* cannot be a property, since it is *to be* that makes possible the existence of any property at all; it is that without which no property whatsoever can be conceived, though it is true that we must be careful to avoid the sort of scheme in which being exists in some way anterior to properties; nothing could be more fallacious than the idea of a sort of nakedness of being which exists before qualities and properties and which is later to be clothed by them. This, of course, has been seen with the utmost clarity by your eighteenth-century thinkers.

We should note in addition that we must establish a most intimate connection between being pure and simple on one side and the being of the copula, the verb of judgment of predication on the other side; though it is not necessarily opposite to being in the sense of the rather hoary distinction between analytic and synthetic judgment. For example, if I say 'This stone is heavy' or 'This stone is white', I am only stressing certain specific aspects of the comprehensive affirmation 'This stone *is*'. One might even say that the judgment of predication is a special viewing of the indestructible reality of the stone which is transposed to the plane of logical affirmation. Remember, too, that we cannot be too distrustful of the examples which appear in treatises on logic; in these the propositions are isolated from their contexts and lose their correct emphasis and precise meaning; they lose, I mean, everything which in concrete reality is conveyed by intonation. For example if I pick up a chair and say 'This chair is heavy!' that is an exclamatory proposition. The exclamation is an integral part of what I say. I do not simply want to say 'This chair has weight'; probably I want to say 'This chair weighs more than I thought, I have a job to lift it!' It is very seldom in the concrete life of thought that I have occasion to make what one could call an affirmation of being; the exceptional case is when a being has made its appearance in the world, has burst into life—a birth, for example, or the completion of a work of art. Then the affirmation becomes a sort of salute or greeting, as though I made a formal acknowledgment of some thing.

There is, of course, another example, a unique one, which we shall have to deal with at length when we come back to it; it is the affirmation which bears upon the existence of God Himself. Whatever audible form this thought may take, there are moments when in effect I say to myself, 'God is': if I am a mystic it may be that I am continually making this affirmation. But what is immediately apparent, and what we shall see more precisely later, is that this affirmation lies beyond every judgment of predication; we may well have to ask ourselves later also how far it is possible for us to have, in regard to the existence of God the partial or incomplete views, I should almost say the sidelights, which we can always get when we are concerned with a particular reality, a reality that can be designated, that is, with a *this*.

But on the other hand, have we not—especially when we have greeted a birth or the appearance of a work of art—used the word *being* in the sense of *existence*? This question of the relation between being and existence has always been a pre-occupation of mine; I may say that it has always worried me. The time has come in these lectures to make a frontal attack on it, and the first thing we must succeed in doing is to find some starting points which are free from ambiguity: we cannot say some definitions, for we are now beyond the limits of the definable. I note that Gilson, at least when he is speaking of St. Thomas Aquinas, has no scruple in identifying being with existence; he translates the formula *ens dicitur quasi esse habens* as 'being is that which has existence' ('*l'être est ce qui a l'exister*'). It is not without reason, he adds, that to that which possesses existence (*esse habens*) is given the name of being (*ens*); in fact the very word *being* is derived from that which designates the act of existing (*esse*). As St. Thomas says '*Hoc nomen ens imponitur ab ipso esse*'. We must understand by that, that the word *ens* which directly and in the first place signifies the thing (*res*), at the same time always signifies the act of existing. The ontology which bears upon *being* conceived in this light rests, then, from the start and of necessity on the firm foundation of essences which are grasped by their concepts and formulated by their definitions; but in the essence which is apt to be conceptualized, this ontology will always keep in view the act of *esse*, of which no concept can be formed, and which is signified by the act of judgment. That is why only judgment, which says what is and what is not, ultimately gets at the truth about things. It arrives at their truth because, in and through their essences, it arrives at their acts of existence.

Without at first committing myself to one side or the other in this matter, I think that we should recall to our minds what we said last year about existence properly so called. Remember in the first place the crucial distinction which I tried to establish between existence and objectivity. Later we shall have to ask ourselves what repercussions that distinction can have on the question of being as we are now considering it. ' The more we lay stress on the object as such,' I wrote in an article, *Existence et Objectivité*, which appeared in 1925 in the *Revue de Métaphysique et de Morale*, 'on the characteristics which, in as much as it is an object, make it up; on the intelligibility with which it must be charged if it is to give a line of approach to the subject which faces it; the more we shall be obliged to leave its existential aspect in darkness. What will be deliberately left out will be the mode according to which the object is present to the person who is considering it; or, which comes to the same thing, the mysterious power of self-affirmation thanks to which the object can present itself before a spectator; and deeper than this will be the question of knowing how it can happen that this object is not simply an inarticulate spectacle, but is endowed also with the power of affecting in countless ways even the being of the person who contemplates it and experiences it. The sensible presence of the thing which, if it is not confused with its existence, seems, at least to unprejudiced reflection, as though it were its manifestation, its most immediate revelation—it is *that* which a philosophy which is directed at once towards ideas and towards objects, tends inevitably to slur over.' When I re-read that passage I seem to detect a certain hesitation, a certain wavering. 'The sensible presence of the thing, which if it is not confused with its existence seems at least to be its most immediate revelation'. What exactly does that mean? I think the effect of the reservation is to keep a sort of gap or interval between something which may be the being of existence or which may simply be its appearance. But I must admit that I should not now be willing to maintain this distinction. I believe on the contrary that to think of existence is ultimately to think of the impossibility of any opposition here between being and appearance : the reason for this became in time more and more apparent to me : it is that the existential aspect is inextricably bound up with my own condition of being not only incarnate but also a wayfarer—*Homo Viator*. When I recognize, when I salute the existence of anything, I recognize at the same time that before a day has gone it will no longer exist, in the sense that I shall no longer myself exist bodily. We can see this most clearly when we consider things which are bound up with human life : the house in which such and such a person was born no longer exists, it was pulled down at such and such a date, nothing remains in its place but elements that have been scattered to infinity, nothing but a handful of dust.

In reality, however, our problem is not quite so simple as it appears at first. Last year I tried to show that there is an *existent*, which serves as a central criterion to which must be referred all the judgments of existence which I may be led to pronounce; this central criterion is my own body, regarded not just as a body, as a corporeal thing, but as my own; or better as a presence whose mass makes itself felt in an all-pervading way. This presence will not, accordingly, allow itself to be reduced, as objects in so far as they are pure objects of knowledge are reduced, either to a simple aspect or to a co-ordination of inter-related aspects. We could put this another way by saying that my body is endowed with a density that is lived or felt; and in so far as I bring other things before myself as existents, I confer on them, too, by analogy, a density of the same order. The complication springs here from the sort of irreducible duality as a result of which the existent is at the same time a thing and yet in some way more than a thing. This is true first of all, of course, of my own body and of other people's bodies. To be more precise, let us note that in so far as my body is subject to accident, it can and should be treated essentially as a thing; to take an example that is unhappily only too familiar to us nowadays, it must be so treated in so far as it can be handled and ill-treated by those who would do it mischief. But we must hasten to add that the happening of these accidents or the infliction of this inhuman ill-treatment can be understood only in so far as the victim is thought of as a subject or, if you like, as a centre. They *happen* to a certain living somebody; nothing could possibly happen to a mere *thing*, because it has no interiority, no life of its own, it is *ownless*. Applied to a thing which was nothing more than a thing, these words would be meaningless.

In these circumstances the use of the words 'to cease to exist' presents a difficult problem. It is true that the thing which has been destroyed, or taken apart, or reduced to dust, has ceased to exist, but in the deepest sense of the word, has it ever existed? Should we not perhaps have good reason to say that it is only to the pseudo-existent (that is, the thing

25

which is nothing more than a thing, which has been wrongly assimilated to my body), that it can happen to cease to exist? In that case how is the question to be applied to the true existent? What do we mean when we say that Victor Hugo or Napoleon no longer exists? To be exact, what we mean is that if we reduce Victor Hugo or Napoleon to a certain mechanism which functioned at a certain time, that mechanism is no longer functioning; it no longer even subsists, in the sense in which a carriage no longer subsists which is worn out and has been sent away as scrap iron.

I have purposely used the word 'mechanism'. While we use that word, we stay in the domain of objects, or rather of what I have called 'things'. But last year we saw that my body is a presence, and in virtue of that it cannot be reduced to being my mechanism, my instrument; I mean that it somehow transcends its being my instrument. I *am* my body, we said, whereas I am not my spade nor my bicycle. But if we take a concrete view of Victor Hugo or Napoleon, if, that is to say, we do not allow ourselves that crude reduction, it is extremely doubtful whether to say that 'they no longer exist' has any meaning at all.

I agree that this analysis is disconcerting; the conclusion to be drawn from it is not an easy one and appears paradoxical. It is that the idea of existence—if it is, anyway, an idea,—is fundamentally involved in an ambiguity. I should even go so far as to say that it is just as though we were faced by something lying on *a slope*; it tends to slide down the slope but at the same time it is precariously held in position—by a thread, perhaps; we are holding the thread and if we pull it, it may just be possible for us to *haul it up* the slope. How do I apply that comparison? In this way: our own inclinations impel us to treat existence as the fact that a thing is *there* and yet could after all be elsewhere, or could even be nowhere at all; to look upon existence in the light of every vicissitude possible in this order, every displacement, every destruction. But if I concentrate my attention on this simple fact: I exist; or again: 'such and such a being whom I love, exists', the perspective changes; to exist no longer means '*to be there* or *to be elsewhere*'; in other words it means that essentially we transcend the opposition between *here* and *elsewhere*. And this is, of course, an illustration of what I said about the necessity of transcending spatial categories.

But are we not beginning to find ourselves again, in this perspective, faced by the embarrassing question of the relation between being and existence? It may well be that there is an ambiguity at the root of existence, and that it is that which makes the problem so difficult. We may consider the existence of a thing regarded only as a thing—the existence which is already, in common with all the others, under the shadow of the threat of 'ceasing to exist'; but we certainly cannot say that it is the existence of non-being; such a statement, I believe, means nothing at all. We shall do better to say that it is scarcely being at all; it is as though it rebelled against the demands which the word 'to be' brings with it. Later we shall have to examine those demands more and more closely. But if on the other hand, we climb up the slope again, existence will seem to us as having ultimately to be indistinguishable from authentic being. I am so bold as to hope that I shall be able to elucidate this later, but I think that a short digression may help us, from now on, to clarify our thoughts. Let us concentrate on the thought of something which no longer exists, in the sense in which the words are commonly used: a garden, perhaps, which has been done away with; in its place a six-

storey house has been built. Is it not obvious that even in this
example there is no way in which we can speak of non-being
in a radical sense? However paradoxical it may seem, as soon
as I can say of the garden, 'it no longer exists', then there is a
certain sense in which it still *is*. I may be accused of playing
on words; it may be urged that it is not the garden which still
exists, it is an image of it which I have preserved. But we
cannot be too careful of the confusions which lurk in the word
'image'. We always tend to think of an image as a sort of
facsimile which has existence, but the idea of a facsimile
implies that something has been materially shaped to resemble
another thing; in that sense the image of the garden *is not* a
facsimile. I do not doubt that there is a way in which the
garden subsists. How? In me? We must be extremely careful,
for here there are worse confusions waiting to ensnare us;
there is the tendency to think of myself as a sort of cupboard
or drawer in which the facsimile may be kept. But the truth
seems to be that these pictorial ways of looking at the matter
should be altogether rejected

At this point I cannot but refer to two of the finest passages
in contemporary literature—Rilke's ninth *Duinese Elegy* and
his own comments on it in a letter to Witold Hulewicz,
written, it appears, on 13 November, 1925. It is No. 108
in the Insel-Verlag edition of the *Briefe aus Muzot*. 'We are
the bees of the invisible. We madly raid the honey of the
visible, to store it in the great golden hive of the invisible.'
When Rilke speaks of 'us' he is, naturally, thinking of poets.
But we may well think—though I do not know whether he
would have accepted the wider interpretation—that every
human being, in so far as he is endowed with memory, shares
in this activity which is proper to the poet: this alchemist's

activity by which the visible is transmuted into the invisible.

Is it not precisely here that we may see how existence and being are dovetailed together?

Another thing emerges with great clarity from this discussion, particularly if we return to the metaphor I used earlier: it is that freedom comes into the picture at precisely the moment when being and existence are in fusion. It is only a free being that can resist the sort of bias which tends to drag it in the direction of the thing, towards the mortality which is inherent in the thing. Without doubt this is not the whole story, but equally without doubt it is by resisting the bias that freedom takes shape.

This way of looking at it is for me an illustration of the great advantage of rejecting the notion according to which existence could be considered as a modality of being; it is a crude notion and it is philosophically untrue. Moreover, to put it in this way would introduce the additional grave embarrassment of the notion that being is a genus. This notion is strictly untenable. More than this, if we were to see in existence a particular specification of being, we should also have to admit that non-existence—we may call it 'absence' if we wish—is another specification of being. But that would be a caricature of relations which are in reality entirely different. Absence can only be apprehended as in any way a mode of being, by the existent, by linking it up with its own existence and as though it were from the depths of its own existence. This comes back to saying that existence and non-existence cannot be treated as terms which are patient, if I may so express it, of being looked at simultaneously in a picture. Every synopsis implies, moreover, that the *looker* shall be at the outside in relation to the thing *looked at*: and such a relation cannot be envisaged in this instance. We can demonstrate this in another way. If we avoid the mistake of treating being and existence as qualities, we shall run the risk of thinking that existence is a sort of specification of a fundamental act; which act would be the act of being. To proceed on these lines would be to meet difficulties which pile up until they are quite unsurmountable.

Can we be quite certain that the words *act of being* are not in some way contradictory? However we may define the word *act*, it is evident that I cannot speak of the act of being unless I am ready to give up the idea of conceiving anything resembling a subject of the act, a *someone* who fulfils the act. We should have to admit that this subject itself *is*, and that would send us back again to a being which is anterior to the act of being. We must, then, lay it down as a principle that the act of being is itself this same subject, but that in some way it is its own creator. Let us admit that we can really think of this creation of self by self. But there does not appear to be anything there which could be regarded as capable of assuming specifications according to various differing modes, of which one would be what we call existence.

However, I think the time has come to leave this rather barren field of speculation, and to address ourselves, as hitherto we have constantly sought to do, to the concrete apprehension of existence. We have reached a point where the question that should concern us lies in knowing whether there is any way in which I can have experience of myself as *being*—being in a sense which is not that in which I can grasp myself as *existing*. When the question is first asked, it seems indeed an obscure one. A little light, I think, is thrown on it only if we stress the actual etymology of the verb 'to exist': if we emphasize, that is, that to exist is to emerge, to arise. But it is clear that if I can somehow rise up so that I become more readily perceived by others, so also I can withdraw myself into my own inner being; that, in fact, is what happens as soon as I am in a state of recollection. This act appears to be bound up with the foreknowledge of a reality which is mine, or perhaps, more exactly, gives me a foundation on which, in as much as I am myself, I can stand: the movement of turning towards this reality helps me to approach it, but it can never enable me fully to coincide with it. If it is true that I can in a certain sense take hold of my own existence, my own being, on the other hand, cannot be an object of my affirmation. We might be tempted to say that there is always a gap between me and my being; I can narrow the gap, it is true, but at least in this life I cannot hope to bridge it. There is an important passage in Charles Du Bos' *Dialogue avec André Gide*, which I think is apposite. Du Bos starts, he says, 'from a faith which has never been shaken, not even in the bosom of religious unbelief: a faith in the existence of the soul on the one hand, and on the other of the constant watch from above which the soul keeps over all the conditions and manifestations of *me*: I am never without the mysterious feeling of the presence and at the same time the distance of the soul at every moment of our life'. 'The presence and at the same time the distance'— it is that sort of telling contradiction which helps me to define my relation to my own being. What Du Bos here calls the soul, is in reality my being: conversely, it must be apparent that the being which we are trying now to close in on can only be qualified as the soul. If that is so, we realize at once with what care the affirmation 'I am' must be approached: the affirmation which was cried on high by Descartes, who thought that he had proved its validity once and for all. I would prefer to say that it should not be put forward in any defiant or presumptuous tone; rather should it be whispered humbly, with fear and wonder. I say *with humility* because, after all, as we shall see more and more clearly, this being is something that can only be granted to us as a gift; it is a crude illusion to believe that it is something which I can give to myself: with *fear*, because I cannot even be certain that I may not make myself unworthy of the gift, so unworthy that I should be condemned to losing it, did not grace come to my assistance: and finally *with wonder*, because this gift brings as its companion the light, because this gift *is light*.

CHAPTER III

ONTOLOGICAL EXIGENCE

A T the end of the last chapter we took up a privileged position from which to consider the relation of being and existence; if we again avail ourselves of the same perspective we shall have to recognize not exactly that the question of their relationship is insoluble, but, more accurately, that it is lost in a cloud of ambiguity. We shall have to note, also, that it would certainly be illusory or misleading to attempt a definite and quite final answer and to say, 'My existence is ordered towards being, I exist in order to be'. This statement is probably not entirely without truth, but it means that we force truth into a scheme which is much too simplified or cut and dried; whereas, on the contrary, the true connection is infinitely more rich, its depths are inexhaustible; and this is true of everything which touches upon being. In any case existence cannot be reduced to a mean or to a collection of means; in reality it comes to us as something which contains and also goes beyond everything to which we might seek to reduce it. But this is not all. We have already seen that the more my existence takes on the character of including others, the narrower becomes the gap which separates it from being; the more, in other words, I am. This amounts to saying that there is no way in which we can conceive of being as something cut off from existence, while it seems almost fatal to

33

picture it to ourselves as an end, or something which is in some respects independent of the means which ensure its realization.

It looks as though the road we are to follow is becoming more defined, and we must follow it a long way further. Last year we saw in detail how difficult it is to throw any light on the depths which I call my past or my life, and what we saw then cannot fail to have a direct effect upon whatever idea I can formulate of my existence, of my *exister*. It is clear that in this connection the possessive adjective *can* and *should* be spiritualized to an increasing degree. There is a sense in which it is literally true to say that the more exclusively it is *I* who exist, the less do I exist; and conversely, the more I free myself from the prison of ego-centricism, the more do I exist. It follows that it would be philosophically absurd to say that my being may be reached through my existence. To the ear of a metaphysician or of a man of spirituality, the words *my being* always have a suspicious sound. It is true that Charles Du Bos speaks of *my soul* in the passage I quoted above, and I thought it opportune to identify provisionally my soul and my being; but I should not hesitate to admit that the words *my soul* are themselves also open to grave objections; I am constantly led to feel that they imply the possession of something which ought to be preserved, enlarged, which ought to be developed. For elementary religious instruction there may be some advantage in the use of the words, but it is clear that if we take a wider view of things, there is a danger of their degenerating into a sort of self-worship which has nothing in common with a religion worthy of the name; in fact it is an extremely dangerous perversion of religion. There are countless metaphors for describing my soul: I may see it as a pearl to be drawn from the depths of the sea, or as a statue to be released from the embrace of the raw stone, or as a garden to be tilled: but from whichever of these angles I look at it, I am in danger of failing to recognize the higher claims of intersubjectivity. To put it in simpler and more ordinary language, which will be more appropriate for what follows, I am in danger of sinning against love.

Even if we agree in general with what I have just said, it is true that, if thought works along these lines, it may be in danger of arriving finally at a de-personalized conception of being; it might look in the end uncommonly like a more or less disguised pantheism. We shall see more clearly as we proceed why there can be no foundation for this fear if we look at it from the point of view I have taken up. But it is well to reject once and for all and in the strongest terms, the idea that in order to avoid pantheism it is necessary to cling to the idea of a human person as rigidly circumscribed as possible. Here again is one of those pictorial representations, which are not only falsifications; they tend to a crude materialism. We have opposed them on countless occasions, and we shall probably again have occasion to point out the truth, which is that if we start from this sort of notion, which is that of ego-centric common sense, God cannot be thought of in any real way; or at least He can be thought of only as an idol and not as a spirit.

At the same time, I am afraid that we may now be in the embarrassing position of a traveller who has left the main road and taken a side turning which he thought was a short cut. When he comes out again into a wider road he is uncertain whether it is the one he left, in fact he *does not know where he is*. In other words, can we be sure that the progress we have made has really been in the right direction? Have we, perhaps, been rash in leaving our enquiry into *being in general* in order to examine what it is I envisage when I speak of *my being*?

We must, of course, note that we have just been obliged to deprive *my being* of the possessive mark which in a manner restricts it. But can we proceed from the point we have reached to a conclusion which embraces being *par excellence*? First of all we must realize the sort of interior resistance or protest with which my method of conducting these investigations is faced.

If we ask ourselves questions about being, are we not putting a question which concerns everything which is, so that the answer should have an universal validity? On the other hand, if we take a short cut as I have done, are we not most arbitrarily narrowing the field of application of the answer?

We must also, I think, concentrate our attention on the postulate which is implied in the objection. The objection rests ultimately on the preconceived idea that the 'being' whose nature we are trying to pin down is something like a predicate which is patient of being ascribed to no matter what. But the words 'no matter what' are significant; or rather they cannot be taken literally. There are things which, it is commonly agreed, do not exist. We need, then, a predicate which can be applied only to things which do exist. But we have already reached the conclusion that that road leads nowhere. Moreover, to take the opposite line and try to treat being as a subject in relation to every possible predicate, will not help us either in the least; on the contrary there is reason to believe, as we shall see later, that we are only wasting our time if we try to conceive of being in its reference to the categories of traditional logic. For if we proceed on these lines, it seems that we are inevitably led to betray the exigence of being: and it is to obtaining a more and more precise consciousness of this that our efforts are directed. Here it is that we find our indirect or negative justification for the attempt we have made to consider first my own being; remembering that it is my *being* and not *my* being which we are considering.

We are accordingly obliged by necessity to recognize that being, in the full sense of the word, cannot be treated as a datum. But we have had ample opportunity to understand also that the exigence of being is not a simple desire or a vague aspiration. It is, rather, a deep-rooted interior urge, and it might equally well be interpreted as an appeal.

In my *Position et Approaches concrètes du Mystère ontologique*, I mentioned, though rather too briefly, this problem; and I may well refer to it now. It has been translated into English and appeared in the collection of papers called *The Philosophy of Existence*. But I should mention that there is one point in which the translation may be misleading. The translation reads: *being is, or should be, necessary*. What I wrote in French was: '*Il faut qu'il y ait ou il faudrait qu'il y eut de l'être*', which is quite a different thing. The *il faut* or the *il faudrait* refers to the exigence that is seated in me. Elsewhere the translator has used the word *need*, and this also distorts my thought somewhat, as it implies something that is *wanted* rather than something that is *demanded*. So that my meaning may be clearer, it will be well to give you the context.

At the beginning of the essay, as in the second of last year's lectures, I noted that the modern misuse of the idea of function tends to debase all human relations. A simple example— a foolish young man, a journalist, put to me quite frankly the idea that the mother of a family should be paid a wage. In other words, her activity should be treated as a function and remunerated as such. The modern worship of the state, again, is simply one aspect of the extension of the notion of function; an extension which is really pathological in its extravagance. The deadly boredom we find in the countries which are stricken by this cancer is bound up with a corresponding weakening of the sense of being, and with an increasing disappearance of joy.

It may be, however, that in that passage, which was written in 1933, I took it rather too much for granted that my readers would understand what I was referring to. The case of the artist is undoubtedly the most illuminating in this context, and it may be as well to start from that.

We cannot be wrong in admitting, even though the meaning of the statement may not be as clear as we should wish, that when any artist whatsoever creates something, he is, in fact, fulfilling a social function; but the trouble arises from the fact that if we stress the social function as such, we are considering his activity from a point of view which cannot and should not be his own; we are looking at the wrong side of it, and I may add that even the existence of the wrong side is problematical. For we must remember that the place for every function is in a certain given economy, and in the general framework of that economy the function is simply a working part. But the artist cannot make his creative activity subservient to anything which is outside himself—except perhaps in the specifically religious field, and in that field the notion of function, which is essentially profane and administrative, loses all significance.

We must go further. From the moment where the artist accepts the notion that he is the performer of a social function, or *a fortiori* a government servant, he abdicates his position, he signifies his readiness to accept every surrender that may be forced upon him in totalitarian countries. That amounts to saying that he ceases to be an artist. But at the same time he makes it impossible for himself to experience anything which approaches the joy of creation; for that joy cannot be divorced from true freedom, our views on which we shall have to express more precisely. To go back, however, to the example I quoted before, surely we can see that there is an intimate relation between artistic activity and the continuous cycle of gestation which is the full realization of motherhood? Even in these days, when so many ideas have run riot, it is difficult to imagine what a mother would be like who thought of herself, in the exercise of her maternal activity, as carrying out a social function. It would be better still, in that view, to take the child from its mother and have it brought up in a state nursery, which would amount to saying that the mother is simply the mechanism by which the child was brought into the world, and that she has accordingly no rights over the child. At least she has as yet the consolation that she will not see herself registered, regimented, and put on duty in an institution. These are, of course, only indications, but we could profitably give many more which would clarify what we are discussing. For example, there is the state nurse who is on duty for so many hours a day, like a lift; when her turn of duty is over, she does not scruple to leave her patient in the lurch, giving the excuse that she does not owe her state employer an extra five minutes; this woman is a state functionary to the marrow of her bones; she has failed to realize that to look after a sick person is something that goes beyond everything that can be defined as a function. Here we may anticipate an objection. It will be urged, I am sure, that the word 'function' may well be used in a less restricted sense and with less of denigration attached to it. After all, does not man's nobility consist in carrying out as well as possible the functions which are proper to him? That question implies that those functions do not necessarily make him into a machine. No doubt: but it is equally true that in a world as complicated as ours, in which division of labour has been pushed to extremes, function has been subdivided also—fragmented, I might say—with the result that it has lost both its value and its interest. In any degree of hierarchy of function you like, you can indeed conceive of beings who fulfil even the most subordinate functions with zeal and intelligence; in fact you have no need to imagine them—there is a very considerable number of such beings. But what is important to recognize is that in such a world the natural tendency becomes stronger and stronger for the individual to treat his function as a task which he cannot put his heart into. His heart, I repeat—a small and simple word, but here it reaches to the essence of the matter. It is perhaps from precisely that angle that we can best consider the problem we have been discussing.

One thing we, or at least some of us, feel acutely: it is this lack of something, this impoverishment, this aridity. We have already seen that it is by starting from that point that we can experience what I have called ontological exigence; but another difficulty may now arise. Is there not reason to fear that what we have found is purely and simply a sort of sentimental condition, to which the philosopher has no right to attach any real metaphysical significance? Is it no more than analogous to the nostalgia we sometimes feel when we recall what life might have been like in the time of stage coaches and oil lamps? In answering these criticisms, we must remember that we can nowadays in no way preserve the opposition between our different faculties which an old-fashioned psychology would try to establish. In his great work *The Meaning of God in Human Experience*, William Ernest Hocking has given an admirable analysis of the matter, and I am glad to quote from it; in his chapter, *The Destiny of Feeling*, he writes: 'All positive feeling, I shall now say, reaches its terminus in knowledge. All feeling means to instate some experience which is essentially cognitive : it is idea-apart-from-its-object tending to become idea-in-presence-of-its-object—which is "cognizance" or experimential knowledge'.* Feeling, after all, is only the sum total of the relatively disconnected phases through which the idea passes in order to take cognizance of itself, in order to be in a position to formulate itself as an idea.

It is true that we do not seem to have made any definite advance; for we still have to ask ourselves whether the idea which reaches embodiment through the voicings of feeling is a true idea; to put it more deeply, whether it is legitimate to speak of truth in connection with such an idea.

We are now directly faced by the notion of value. An overfunctionalized world seems to us to be lacking in something, judged by the standard of certain values—and those values we should define more precisely. But are they not themselves very different from what we call truth? We could put the question even more simply. There are people who are dismayed by the idea that humanity is tending towards a type of civilization in which reduction to a level will be the rule, in which the advantages which the past has accorded to the comfort and mode of life of a privileged class are doomed to disappear: but can this dismay and regret be given any

*Yale University Press, 1922, pp. 67-68.

metaphysical significance? Is it not just a matter of preferences, of an order whose statements are of the type 'I like' and 'I do not like'? You must note that we have imperceptibly shifted from what should be the consideration of being to the consideration of truth. Should we really have avoided that change of ground? I can hardly believe it. It is surely impossible for us not to have at any rate a vague assurance that being can only nominally be distinct from a certain fullness of truth. That fullness is in contrast with the partial, specialized, truths to which it is difficult to attach any ontological import. The word 'fullness' which I have just used is extremely important, but it must not be understood quantitatively, as though it implied the total of a sum. Of such a totality we might well enquire whether it is not a sort of a pictorial representation of fullness, whereas in fullness there is something which cannot be pictured, which will not tolerate such a projection. Is it not the need for this fullness which gives us a starting point to throw light on the problems we are discussing in this chapter? It is the fullness which is the contradiction at once of the hollowness of a functionalized world and of the overpowering monotony of a society in which beings take on more and more the appearance of specimens which it is increasingly difficult to differentiate.

The objection which we considered before comes back now in a very similar form. When we commend or condemn things in this way, are we not doing so at the instance of something which is only an ideal, only the aspiration of an incurably romantic sentimentality? Once more, it seems, we are back in the realm of pure subjectivity.

But this is precisely where secondary reflection should come in. We must certainly ask ourselves what we mean when we speak of mere subjectivity, and consider what is its opposite. It is clear that we distinguish the ideal, regarded as something more or less nebulous, from the hard reality of fact: the latter is the firm ground on which we stumbling creatures tread our painful road.

We must consider, also, whether we are not confusing the ideas of fact and factitious, whether, that is, we are not shifting into a plane which is really that of value and freedom; of a freedom, however, which turns against itself and provides its own negation. This is what happens when a cynical old realist argues with his revolutionary grand-children. He opposes the real world of vested interest to the reign of social justice which the grandchild would inaugurate: he imagines that he has fact on his side, but in reality he is supporting a world of vested interest which he thinks he can treat as a permanent physical or perhaps biological reality. There are different ways in which such a position may be taken up. One may be an active accomplice, or one may simply be resigned and acquiesce. But in any case it seems that what we have is simply a pseudo-reality which is presented to the will before the latter can even exercise its proper function.

All this certainly applies to the functionalized world. Such a world can exist only in so far as it is willed and accepted. But a man may be involved in that world and yet retain the power to reject it. He rejects it in the degree to which he succeeds in humanizing the relations which unite him to his superiors, to his equals and, most of all, to his inferiors. We have reason, therefore, to think that the traditional opposition between fact and ideal is, in this context, an illusion and that it misses out the essence of the matter. We might even make use also of the idea of a counter-value, which the realist affixes like a stamp or seal to the reality of the fact whose self-sufficiency he attempts to proclaim. But a *counter-value* cannot be thought of without a value; it presupposes it.

Even so, we cannot yet solve the difficult problem of discovering the relations between value and being. One thing now seems reasonably clear: *being* cannot, it is certain, be indifferent to *value*; it could only so be if one were to identify it as a crude datum considered as existing in its own right, and that we are not justified in doing; in fact we must resolutely reject the idea of the existence in its own right of such a crude datum. The datum can only be grasped—René Le Senne has seen this very clearly—as an obstacle against which something hurls itself, and this something is not included in the datum; it will be found to spring, rather, from desire or aspiration. It will be legitimate, then, to say in a certain sense that where there is an experience of being, it is always a direct contradiction of this consciousness of a divorce between the datum and the aspiration. I once wrote, 'Being is the culmination of hope, the experience of being is its fulfilment'. The retort may be made that there is room after all, even in the world of the purely functional, for fulfilment. But in what does it consist? Most often it consists in having got through a task which is nothing but a task, with which, that is to say, there can be no interior identification. Let us imagine that I have answered so many letters today, or that I have sent out so many circulars in my day's work. It is true that I have done my work, but it has not been very different from a ticket collector punching tickets, or even a machine making so many revolutions. The human machine, indeed, is conscious of itself as a machine, and to that extent it is more than a machine, but there is no more real creation with one than with the other. I may add, to keep the thread of my argument clear, that any functionalized activity is manifestly the lowest depth of degradation to which creative activity can descend; and I cannot stress too emphatically that the word 'fulfilment' can take on a positive meaning only from the point of view of creation. Moreover, it is clear, as we have already suggested, that creation is not necessarily the creation of something outside the person who creates. To create is not, essentially, to produce. There can be production without creation, and there can be creation without any identifiable object remaining to bear witness to the creation. I think that we must all, in the course of our lives, have known beings who were essentially creators; by the radiance of charity and love shining from their being, they add a positive contribution to the invisible work which gives the human adventure the only meaning which can justify it. Only the blind may say with the suggestion of a sneer that they have produced nothing. Even so, when we say that being is fulfilment, are we perhaps still entangled in an ambiguity? The formula does not seem likely to satisfy a mind which insists on strict accuracy. The question is whether fulfilment can be considered on its own, or whether on the contrary it is involved in the life of a consciousness which finds in fulfilment something to satisfy a profound requirement. There is no doubt that the latter is the correct alternative. But if we do look at fulfilment in this light, shall we not find that it corresponds to what is only a phase in a development, and that this development involves, in relation to the fulfilment, a something which is this side of it and a something which lies beyond it—a preparation, a growth, but also a dissolution? Such an idea, which is after all relativist, can hardly be entertained if we identify being and fulness. It would seem better to admit that what we have called fulfilment should be interpreted in this context as a mode of participation in . . .—it is extremely difficult to find a definite word to fill this gap; or rather, although we can always avoid it by using an abstract word, there is a danger that the abstraction will be simply a stopgap. What does seem to emerge is that the problem presents itself very differently according to whether we *are* or *are not* in the domain of the spiritual. It is only analogically true to say of a plant which blossoms or fruits that it participates in the reality, the strictly ineffable reality, to which our tortuous and troublesome enquiry is directed. Without going into the almost insoluble complications contained in the theological notion of analogy, we may perhaps be content to say that the fulfilment realized in the flower or the fruit, is such only for an appreciating consciousness which apprehends the flower as a flower and the fruit as a fruit. Here the intervention of the appreciating consciousness is necessary for the fulfilment to be recognized as such; but this fulfilment is interiorized as soon as we enter the domain of either personal or inter-personal intersubjectivity. Now, perhaps, we can better understand why ontology, as we saw before, demands for its definition the addition of the dimension of intersubjectivity to that of objective knowledge. We could, in fact, say that fulfilment as such is meaningless if it is considered from the angle of an objective or descriptive knowledge. And so we meet again the mysterious dovetailing (or articulation—I should use the same word in French) of being and value which we noticed before.

We must not, however, be misled by this word 'dovetailing' itself, as though we were concerned with a connection between two concepts that can be presented for our consideration; on the contrary, we must, I believe, be clear from the start that to look at things in this light will never lead us to any conclusion that will be metaphysically satisfactory. The peculiarly disconcerting nature of our enquiry rests upon just this point, that when we speak of *being*, we cannot but project before ourselves some sort of schema—however abstract it may be—and yet at the same time we must free ourselves from this very projection, we must recognize and expose its illusory nature. In my first series of lectures, I discussed the question of the exigence of transcendence, and you will realize that this is simply the conclusion we then reached.

There is, however, a traditional notion which dominates classic ontology, and it may be appropriate to introduce it at this point. I refer to the notion of perfection. At the same time we must consider whether the word perfection does not always fundamentally involve, explicitly or not, a reference to an activity which is plastic in its essence. The perfect thing is first of all essentially a work which has taken on its final and definitive form, a completed work and, we may well add, a *work which presents itself as such to the observer.* From that angle there is no doubt that it is easier to speak of the perfection of a statue or of a building than of a symphony, for example. But we must nevertheless realize that even here a certain abstract transposition is possible; in that case the judgment of perfection has reference to conformity with a certain canon, and this canon can be conceived without there being, properly speaking, any representation of it. Thus it is that one may praise the perfection of a fugue. But everything goes to show that the praise will refer rather to the construction of the fugue than to the quality of the motif on which it is based. It would be ridiculous to say of the motif that it is perfect; one should even perhaps say that its intrinsic quality lies outside the judgment of perfection properly so called; and this because it belongs much more to the order of the lived than to that of the represented or conceived.

Must we then conclude that the notion of perfection is in reality bound up with a static view of the world? Push the matter to extremes, and it might be possible to admit that conclusion, but not without qualification. I have just quoted the fugue as an example of something which can attain perfection, and the fugue is not static in itself; what we can say is that it lends itself to that act by which we make ourselves a schematic and to some extent figurative representation of it.

I chose the fugue as an example because it belongs to the specifically aesthetic order, but one could as well take a geometric proof. Such a proof can obviously be perfect, and in this case we can attach a precise meaning to the word 'perfect'. It is perfect in so far as it is not only compelling but also as simple as possible; which amounts to saying that it is neither vague nor extravagant—it is 'well-cut' in the sense we speak of clothes as being well-cut.

These examples help us to see the quality of being shut in, of being contained within oneself, which is involved in the notion of perfection. Perfection is self-sufficient, it has no need to send us on to something beyond itself. The theologians, indeed, have tried to reconcile the notions of the perfect and the infinite, but I should personally be inclined to think that this attempt is self contradictory, whereas when the ancients were so taken up by the nature of what is the τέλειον, their depreciation of the infinite showed a fidelity to a deep-rooted logic. We might well, it is true, involve ourselves at this point in complicated developments, for in so far as the infinite of the moderns is a matter for mathematical speculation, it ceases to be the infinite of the ancients, it is no longer in any sense the ἄπειρον of the Greeks. But we may well doubt whether the differential calculus has any appreciable bearing on the problem with which we are now concerned, that is to say on the ontological plane. What does seem to emerge at this point is that to attempt to define being by perfection is in the end to run the risk of reducing it to no more than an abstract representation of itself. But when we spoke of fulfilment, it was not quite on the ground of form as form that we were taking our stand. It was rather that we envisaged what I called an experience of fulness, like that which is involved in love, when love knows that it is shared, when it experiences itself as shared. From this point of view to fulfil is not strictly speaking to accomplish, if by accomplishment we mean that something is finished or brought to a close; for we have seen that fulness is not to be confused with totality. With perfection, however, there is always the danger that it may be interpreted as a whole closed in on itself; indeed I should readily agree that in this respect the idea of perfection leads to a blind alley. Philosophers in the past have always been tempted down this blind alley, and theologians are never quite safe from the same temptation, unless they are wary of the snares of abstract representation.

These remarks, indeed, are purely critical: but they lead us to a point where we can match them with a subtle question. If we posit being as incapable of being reduced to what presents itself to us as perfection or totality, are we not ultimately refusing to posit it at all, that is, shortly, to substantify it? We have been struggling with almost insoluble difficulties; does not the root of these difficulties lie in our obstinate determination to speak of *being*, while at the same time we deprive this being of the characteristics which are essential to its make-up? Even a cursory examination of the *ens realissimum* which has been the core of traditional ontology, will show us clearly the vastness of the problem. The *ens realissimum* is thought of as concentrating all positive attributes in itself; it is like a solid flawless mass, which in some ways might make you think of the sphere of Parmenides—though the philosophers who make it the heart of their thought are by no means Eleatics, preferring no doubt stages of being to the crude alternatives of 'to be' or 'not to be'. But we may well entertain grave doubts of the validity of the mental process which forms the *ens realissimum*, for in this process not only are attributes themselves treated as things, but they are in addition assimilated to elements which are capable of building up a whole. Here more than anywhere else we can see how the idea of totality can be misused. Bergson has said with admirable lucidity that there can be totalization only of that which is homogeneous; it is not by any means everything that can be treated as a unity susceptible of being added to other unities, though there can be no totalization where such an addition is not feasible. In no sense can either a chord or a melody be regarded as wholes of which the notes are elements. To believe that they can be is to have lost sight of the individual, qualified, reality of the chord or of the melody, substituting for it a *schema* which has no more relation to the melody than an anthropometric gauge has to the pictorial essence of a human face.

What is true of an individual being is true *a fortiori* of a universal being which the scholastics claim to reach through their clumsy abstract denominations: the contrary belief depends entirely upon the degree to which one keeps at the root of his thought the almost unacknowledged and obsolete idea that this universal being is generic. We must, indeed, agree with Spinoza's criticism of knowledge of the second genus; we must realize that to affirm being is absolutely to transcend 'knowledge by genus and species'.

These considerations lend even more point to the question we put. Without using the words necessarily in the scholastic sense, we may now say that the object of our enquiry is being *par excellence*; but we must also admit that, in as much as it is being, this being refuses to allow itself to be posited as an object, as a *quid*, as something which can be garnished with a given number of predicates. On the other hand, if it is not a *quid*, if, that is, it is not a predicable, can we legitimately speak of it at all?

CHAPTER IV

THE LEGITIMACY OF ONTOLOGY

AT the end of the last chapter we reached the point where
we had to consider whether the root of the difficulty with
which we were faced did not lie in our being inclined to substantify something which is essentially impatient of being so
treated. We asked ourselves whether this treatment was legitimate.

In the field in which we are engaged, however, the actual
meaning of the word *legitimate* is by no means clear, and we
must first try to define it more precisely.

In a general way we might say that the legitimate is defined
by conformity with a standard that has already been laid down.
But all that we have said of the peculiar and venturesome
nature of metaphysical enquiry should prepare us to doubt the
possibility of affirming such standards in this context; the
principle of contradiction is operative only in the conduct of
a thought in general. I do not mean that we may safely go
against it, but that it retains only a formal value. The truth
appears rather to be that what we need is something which
will provide a starting point from which we may arrive at
some standards. But if this is so, there is a danger that we may
sink into an absolute indeterminism, in which we shall be at
the mercy of all the whims of improvisation.

However, our instinct tells us that it cannot and should not
be so. Nothing must allow our enquiry to be without a definite

orientation; I might say that just as in any other kind of exploration we must steer a compass course. But what is the point of orientation? By what pole can we check our heading? In other words, what must we have before our eyes to ensure that our course is not haphazard? I believe that our point of reference can be based only upon experience itself, treated as a massive presence which is to be the basis of all our affirmation. At the same time we must add that this massive presence of experience, looked at in the indivisible multiplicity of its different aspects, is not an idea to which we should *conform*: we should rather look at it as something which should be taken into account by whoever is intent, I shall not say upon grasping being (for by now it must be abundantly clear that being can never be the object of such a grasp), but upon undertaking a concrete approach to being. Most important of all, we must note that if experience is looked at in this light, it is opposed to all specification, of whatever nature, which is isolated from other specifications: the economic aspect, for example, as it appears from a narrowly marxist point of view; examples of similar abstractions could be taken from pure biology, psychology, or sociology.

We have been forced to use the word 'approach', which is too spatial in significance; and we must guard against the temptation to take it literally. In the first series of lectures, we were able to see that the opposition between outward and inward, or even between near and far, cannot in the metaphysical domain be retained just as it is; and it will gradually become more apparent that the reality which is our most direct concern can in no way be likened to something which we can touch or reach. It is just as much something infinitely distant, infinitely remote and at the same time quite near, on the verge of immediacy; and it is only by accepting this paradox at the outset that we can hope to reach any understanding of faith. In a general way we might say that in the difficult country in which we have to force our way, it is the disjunctive judgment whose inadequacy becomes increasingly apparent; even though it cannot be replaced by a juxtaposition of terms simply united by the words 'also' or 'as well as'. The idea of tension on which Kierkegaard laid such emphasis is the actual mainspring of the type of thought which we now need to set in motion.

I fear that we may seem to be getting more and more befogged. If we cease to speak of being *par excellence*, of being in itself, and direct ourselves to the consideration of beings in particular, might we not hope to emerge with some more intelligible propositions? At this point it seems difficult to avoid the substantification whose legitimacy, in the case of being *par excellence*, seemed to be doubtful. Accordingly, we can now, I think, envisage several hypotheses.

1. Must it be admitted that substantifying is legitimate for what we call particular beings, but *not* for being in itself?

2. Must it, in spite of appearances, be denounced as illegitimate in the one case just as in the other? Or will it, on the contrary, be appropriate, quite paradoxically and in spite of what we have said to the contrary, in spite of everything, to say that it is only as related to being in itself that it is legitimate, and that for beings in particular it is illegitimate?

3. Would it be better simply to sanction in either of the two cases the use of the substantive in current speech?

What is most important of all is to be fully aware of the line we should have to take if we refused to treat any particular being as genuine being. This would no doubt amount to functionalizing it completely, or again to reducing it to a certain type of conduct—we think immediately of prisons or concentration camps in which the individual is known simply by a reference number. A less tragic example is the hotel in which the traveller is hardly distinct from his room number—he is 'the man in number so and so!' In such cases emphasis is systematically diverted from the subject as a subject and laid exclusively on a job to be done, a return to be produced, a bill to be paid. In ordinary life there is nothing to prevent me from behaving to other people in a way which corresponds to this quite pragmatic way of looking at them. Servants are an obvious example. But a husband, after all, can treat his wife as a servant; a father his son, and so on. In these instances we cannot help seeing the real suppression of the value of being. But what we realize at the same time is that it cannot be so suppressed without involving a ghastly mutilation of human relations; we may put it more strongly and say that these human relations entirely lose their specific character. So this by-road has brought us back again to intersubjectivity.

It is interesting to notice, incidentally, that the importance of names comes out clearly in this context. It is apparent that the surname is not simply a sign. It is the individual being's inalienable property; from that point of view one cannot but protest against the habit of certain housewives, at least in France, of always giving the same name (usually Marie) to their successive maids, not to be bothered to remember their real names. It seems that the name lies at the intersection, so to speak, of being and having. It signals more than it signifies the unique place which belongs to the individual in the whole in which he has to find his place and discover the type of creative activity, however limited, which is his own.

Starting from these very concrete considerations, we have

good grounds to infer that it is not quite possible to de-substantify individual beings. This de-substantification remains possible, it is true, less in words than in acts, but this possibility exists as a temptation, and you can see quite clearly nowadays the consequences which are bound to occur when one yields to it.

But under these conditions it is the first hypothesis which we have to face. The problem might be put in the following terms: is it conceivable that *beings* exist in a universe of such a nature that it might be possible at the same time to say '*being is not*'? Let us note immediately that we should be careful in using the word 'universe' in this context. It might be better put: is it or is it not a contradiction to admit that there are *individual beings* and at the same time that *being* as such does not exist?

But first mark well another point: can we say that there are individual beings in the sense in which we say that there is such and such an object, such a piece of furniture, for example, in this room? Such objects can be listed, they can be counted. Human beings, no doubt—and it is with them that we are concerned—can also be calibrated and numbered. Theoretically one could catalogue all the human beings on this planet, in the same way as one could catalogue all the pieces in a collection. But we cannot but realize that if beings are treated in this way, if, that is to say, we force them into an inventory, they are no longer looked at completely as beings, but rather as things. You might urge that this hardly matters: even if I can ascribe being only to those individuals who have not been presented to me in the same way as the tables and chairs in this room, yet as far as I am concerned there are still such privileged beings. The French and German phrases—*il y a, es gibt*—are particularly useful in helping us to grasp the point.

One might perhaps be justified in saying that things (or beings in so far as they can be assimilated to things, in so far as they are nothing but things) are designed with a view to our attention. We have to take them into account, and to do so moreover in a most material way, taking them as obstacles which we must push aside or circumvent. But we give them being, we acknowledge them as being, only from the moment when they become for us, in no matter what degree, centres or focal points, when they evoke in us a reaction of love and respect, or a contrary reaction of fear or even horror. The latter reactions deserve a special study; from the ontological point of view there is some sort of contradiction in their character.

In any case, as soon as beings are looked at in this perspective, as soon, that is, as they are looked at as centres, they can no longer be introduced as simple unities in totalities; therein lies the difficulty of reconciling the feelings, not patient of a common measure, which are aroused in us by beings which we love simultaneously—our wives, children, mistresses. Even when reconciliation is possible, it invariably presupposes considerable difficulty on both sides, there is always a painful adjustment to be effected; it involves a struggle against the sort of ego-centricism I brought up in the first chapter. I need a word to describe these conglomerations which are not totalities, and I shall henceforward, if such a word is needed, call them 'constellations'.

However, we are still no nearer to answering the question on the substantification of being, considering the substantification in relation to that of individual *beings*.

If we are to make any progress, we should, I think, realize distinctly the concrete meaning of refusing to substantify being as such. It is not certain that such a refusal may be interpreted in a strictly univocal sense, but taken sufficiently deeply it assumes the character of a radical metaphysical nihilism.

In this context I have often quoted the words of one of Claudel's characters in *La Ville*:

'Nothing is . . .
Listen: I shall repeat the word I have said: Nothing is.
I have seen and I have touched
The horror of uselessness, I have added the proof of my hands to that which is not.
The Nothing does not lack the power to announce itself by a mouth which can say: I am.
This is my prey, this I have disclosed.'

What is the meaning in that passage of 'Nothing is'? It means precisely that nothing resists, or could resist, the proof of critical experience. Besme does not seem to be asking himself whether the mouth by which the Nothing announces itself *is* or not; or, I should rather say, he is obliged to integrate the mouth itself within the Nothing; and as it is a mouth of flesh and blood, and so perishable, the *nothing* will engulf it. But it is only too clear that there will always be room to enquire how something, which in itself is only an ephemeral modality not, let us say, of being but rather of non-being, can be capable of proferring a universal affirmation—even if the affirmation is only that of the Nothing.

But what we cannot fail to see is that the nihilist affirmation, 'Nothing is', cannot, as we have just seen, be without repercussions on the actual idea of individual beings which we have to form for ourselves. To say, 'Nothing is', is actually to say, 'No being is, there are no individual beings'. Looked at in this way, I shall be forced to recognize that what I took for a being was in reality only the phantom of being, the deceptive imitation of a being; it being necessarily implied that a true being would not be subject to this general law of dissolution.

There is thus a way of affirming the *nothing* which abolishes individual beings as such. But can we not extricate ourselves from this brutal and implacable logic without, in so doing, falling into a contradiction?

A preliminary note seems necessary: what we see is that individual beings are liable to decay; this is precisely what can induce our thought to push itself, by a sort of rash over-reaching, to the fullest limit and to announce that being does not exist, that is to say, that there is nothing of which it can be asserted that it is indestructible or eternal. Looked at in this way, there can be no question of maintaining the reality of individual beings. On the contrary it is this reality which is the first to be denied and overwhelmed or swallowed up. But we still need to know whether it is legitimate thus to assert at the outset the non-reality of individual beings.

It would be well to examine whether this initial position does not involve a postulate which should be made more explicit on reflection. This postulate might be briefly expressed as follows: that which perishes partakes visibly of the nature of clouds and shadows; the latter can only be appearances, appearances on the surface of—yes, on the surface of what? Must we admit that what we have are only ephemeral and illusory modalities of a reality whose substantial character we are nevertheless obliged to proclaim? This, you see, is the contrary of what it seemed just before that we should assert; the non-reality of individual beings would now be balanced by the reality of being in itself. We can, however, easily appreciate that thought is more or less obliged to waver indefinitely between these two interpretations; and in the end we may find that there is only a nominal distinction between the two. By that I mean that a thing which in one set of circumstances is treated as *being* can equally well be qualified as *non-being*. The truth of this, moreover, may be seen by the evidence of countless mystics and philosophers: to take a contemporary example, some commentators on Heidegger have professed, not without a certain show of reason, that what he now calls 'Being' (*Sein*) has an odd resemblance to what in his earlier works he called 'Non-being' (*Nichts*). Such a remark seems somewhat hazardous to me, and I should not rely upon it too much; but I should still say that the indecision of thought probably arises from not expressing the problem with enough precision; and we shall have to clarify our appreciation of its significance. When we are dealing with an individual being, apprehended in its quality of being—*loved, that is to say*, for such a description cannot be divorced from the act of loving—then the meaning of the word 'perish' is by no means clear. We can go further: there are very cogent reasons for thinking that the verb 'perish' can by no means be used in this context, if it signifies what happens when a cloud disperses or a flame is extinguished. Those are physical processes, and they can be described in the language of objective knowledge; but if, as we have constantly insisted, it is true that ontology is bound up with intersubjectivity, then those processes can find no place in the ontological order.

The fruit of these remarks is that we must revise the terms in which we formulated the hypotheses put forward at the beginning of the chapter. The faulty character of the formulae depends precisely from the fact that the expressions we used were those which we should have used if we were dealing with an *object*, if it were a question of knowing whether *there was* or was not a compact, massive block of being, which one could call being in itself.

The fact, however, that being cannot be separated from the exigence of being, must never be lost sight of. Therein lies the fundamental reason for the impossibility of severing being from value. Looking at it from this point of view we see that the problem round which our recent enquiries have revolved lies in finding the answer to the question whether the exigence of perennialness is or is not involved in the exigence of being, or whether on the contrary the two exigencies can be separated from one another. Our analysis of the problems of existing and ceasing to exist has, in fact, led us to recognize that the bond between the two cannot be broken. 'To say that one loves a being', says one of my characters, 'means, "Thou, at least, thou shalt not die."' But the only reason, we must emphatically repeat, why such a statement can have any meaning is that love is not something which can be grafted on the affirmation of being. Moreover, we must have a more precise idea of what we mean by the perennial. In this context can perenniality be looked at as a simple perpetual continuation? That would be a rash statement; for the idea of continuation itself is full of ambiguity. Experience shows us that certain creatures—I do not want to use the word 'beings'—are subject to what are real metamorphoses. But can metamorphoses be considered a continuation? When we speak of continuation, we presuppose, I think, a certain minimum preservation of identity as regards the manner of existence; when this minimum is lacking, we cannot be certain of the continuation. For my part, I should rather be inclined to give a negative defininition of perenniality: the real meaning of 'to say that one loves a being is to say, "Thou, at least, thou shalt not die" is rather 'Because I love you, because I affirm you as being, there is something in you which can bridge the abyss that I vaguely call "Death." We still have a certain ambiguity: these formulae, I fear, may have too subjectivist a tone; the emphasis is placed on the affirmation itself or on the assertion itself as such, and not on the thing which is affirmed. Here we reach the crucial part of this involved enquiry: from the moment when my affirmation becomes love, it resigns in favour of that which is affirmed, of the thing which is asserted in its substantial value. This is precisely what love is; it cannot be divorced from this resignation. In other words, love is the active refusal to treat itself as subjective, and it is in this refusal that it cannot be separated from faith; in fact it is faith. And the function of secondary reflection will consist essentially in demonstrating that the refusal is transcendent in relation to the criticism to which primary reflection would claim to subject us.

From another angle, however, could we not say that, judged in the light of rational thought, this refusal must appear as a monstrous claim, as a violation of the very conditions of existence?

We must concentrate on this question; and it is only by finding an answer to it that we shall find a solution to this chapter's enquiry into the legitimacy of an ontology, or in other words of substantification regarded purely as such. Last year we reached certain conclusions about the true nature of reflection and the impossibility of reducing it to a process of analytical dissection. These conclusions, too, we must now use. If we can throw some light, accordingly, on the hidden affinities between secondary reflection and thought, we shall be able to settle our worries.

I have often found it useful to take one of my plays as a starting point. *Le Palais de Sable* seems to me today to anticipate in many ways all my later philosophical development. What I can see in it is like a privileged inner experience, and it gives me a starting point from which the problems can be looked at in their sharpest form and with the utmost precision.

The action takes place in a French provincial town, shortly before the first world war. The principal character, Moirans, is a politician. He is a conservative and his line is the defence of Catholicism against the growth of laicism. He is opposed to the divorce of one of his daughters, and this on the grounds of the traditional ideas which he champions. But an unforeseen development forces him into conflict with the attitude which he has consistently adopted. The only one of his children for whom he feels real tenderness is his other daughter, Clarissa; she tells him that she has decided to become a nun, a Carmelite. Moirans is horrified at the idea and tries to dissuade her. If his faith is real, however, should he not be glad that his favourite daughter has decided to consecrate herself to God ?

Clarissa is appalled at the warmth and passion with which he fights what she thought her vocation; and Moirans is forced to realize that his feeling for religion, for a religious frame of mind and tradition, is not real faith; as soon as a being he loves is concerned, he can no longer bear the idea; suddenly it seems to him meaningless and empty. He is thus made to recognize that fundamentally he does not believe in the other world in which her sacrifice would bring her an everlasting reward. That is not all. He goes further and asserts that such a belief, held as it might be held by simple souls, seems to him childish and mythological. He is thinking in fact as an idealist, and he flatters himself that he has seen through the illusion. Clarissa is overwhelmed by what she learns. Her father seems to her now to be an impostor, a swindler—after all he has always spoken and behaved as though he really believed in what he is repudiating. But at the same time she feels as though she herself were contaminated by this destructive idealism. There is a gap between her faith and herself, and she feels that she can no longer be at one with it. Thus she is led to question her own belief, and finally she wonders whether she has mistaken a temptation for a vocation; whether her desire to take the veil was simply an easy way out of the troubles and dangers of life in the world.

She is deeply disturbed, and consults her spiritual director. But he has no idea of what she is trying to say. 'A nun's life', he says, 'is a hard one. There are many renunciations. You will have to get up in the middle of the night to go to the Chapel, and so on. How could you be yielding to a temptation by believing the convent to be your vocation?' She means that spiritually it can be easier to shut oneself up in such a life, however hard, than to face the world and its temptations. But there is more to be said—Clarissa now feels that she is in some way responsible for her father. She cannot bear her father's continuing in his pose as a champion of the Catholic faith. She begs him to give up political life. His answer is that he will do so if she will give up her plan of entering the convent.

Her conflict increases in intensity. A contradiction asserts itself between what she has always believed to be her vocation and what now seems to her to be a duty whose call she cannot disobey. Things are such that the new duty must surely win the fight—that amounts to saying that she can no longer feel her vocation or believe that she is called. Clarissa is now cut off from what she believed the better, the purer, part of herself. She yields to her father's blackmail, and we see her and Moirans dragging through a life which has ceased to have any meaning for her. She refuses to marry a man whom she loves and respects; she no longer belongs either to heaven or to earth, she is just a shadow.

As for Moirans, he realizes something which astonishes and appals him. He finds that it is impossible for a man, contrary to what he had thought, to shut himself up within himself, to live simply in his thoughts or in what he would like to be his thoughts. As soon as one loves or is loved by another being, an awesome solidarity comes into being between the two. Moirans has been helpless to prevent his daughter's dependence on him; he has been obliged accordingly to yield her a most dreadful power, and has lost for ever all feeling of exaltation; he is no longer his own master, no longer even simply his own property. Everything goes to show, however, that the real core of the drama is the question of the relations between faith and reflection.

The sublime spontaneity of faith has so filled Clarissa's being that she does not struggle against her father's infectious unbelief. It is infectious, it is true, but only because Moirans has always been to her the champion of religion, and, paradoxically, it is his influence which helped to rouse her first ardour. To Moirans, however, Christianity was simply an object of a sort of delight; if he could look on himself as a Christian it was simply because he had been filled with an appreciation of its aesthetic beauty and at the same time of its social utility. It was only the shock that he felt when faced by Clarissa's decision that could make him understand that faith is a very different matter. This links up, I think, with

Maurice Blondel's criticism of dilettantism in *L'Action*.

One might say that in *Le Palais de Sable* reflection appears as a power of critical dissection: but if that is so, it is only because it does not go beyond the primary stage, and is a long way from the corrective function which I defined last year. One might nevertheless say that it is the function proper to drama to arouse secondary reflection in us; and that means precisely to lead us to recognize the misleading character of an idealism whose claim is to have got the better of what it calls the realist illusion.

Thus one may see fairly clearly how secondary reflection, while not yet being itself faith, succeeds at least in preparing or fostering what I am ready to call the spiritual setting of faith.

But what can we say of Moirans' influence on his daughter, which I spoke of as a contamination? We may well be inclined to say that such a word is incorrect and unjust, and that what Clarissa received from her father was his clarity of vision, with the result that what seemed to her to be a fall, should rather be looked upon as a step forward on the road to truth.

It is hardly necessary to emphasize the extreme importance of this question. I might even say that all our future enquiries will be governed by our anxiety to find an answer to it.

We can now see, I think, that if belief lays itself open to the attack of critical reflection, it is because of the aspect which it turns towards it. We can put it more clearly by saying that the determining factor here is the idea which I tend to form of it for myself, or which another tends to form for me, from the moment when I am, or the other is, outside faith: that is from the moment when we cease to live it.

From this outside point of view (and we shall do well to stress that every point of view as such is an outside one) to believe means to imagine that, to have an idea in your mind that. When any of those phrases are applicable, reflection will almost inevitably be seen to be an attempt at re-ordering or straightening. It is in this light that we must inevitably look at a negative criticism of faith. Fundamentally this criticism acts by reduction; it attempts, that is, to oppose a solid reality to the delusions which the power of the affections—desire, generally, and fear—substitute for reality. Such a criticism will invariably tend towards affirmations of the type, 'What you have thought to be *this* is in reality nothing but *that*'. The line of secondary reflection will have to be directed precisely against this reducing thought, for its proper function consists above all in asking whether the idea of faith with which primary reflection was concerned may not be a corrupt or deformed experience of something of an entirely different order.

CHAPTER V

OPINION AND FAITH

IF I am to develop the hints which I suggested at the end of the last chapter, I shall have to resume the analysis of opinion and faith with which I have been concerned in my former books. I have noticed that, at all events with modern thinkers, there is a most distressing tendency for the two to be confused. I began to realize this during the agonizing years just before the second war. I felt that a catastrophe was imminent, and that in it everything I loved might perish; and I said to myself that there was nothing to stop what I thought would be the worst of all calamities. I may add, incidentally, that no one can look at the world today and not have the same feeling. Then I considered what was happening to my faith. I no longer felt it in me as a living reality, it seemed to me to be so devitalized that it was reduced simply to an *opinion* which I knew to be part of my mental equipment, nothing more. I argued the matter with myself. I cannot wilfully shut my eyes, I said: there is a sort of optimism which I cannot force myself to share, because to do so would seem to me to run counter to a certain probity of mind. I can have no guarantee against the destruction of what I love. In those days I used to discuss things with a Catholic who was animated by a very profound faith, but at the same time was a man of exceptional clarity of mind. At first I was annoyed at the calm way in which he took the menace of danger, but I soon realized that it did not come from indifference, and in the end I saw that he indeed had true faith, because he had peace. Later we shall meet again this connection I found between peace and faith, and make what I may call a new harmony of it. But I realized also that I could recognize true faith in him only in so far as there was true faith in me; as in my own case, it was like a plant but at a much earlier stage of development. I took great comfort from this thought.

It was this sort of crisis that led me to examine the nature of opinion, and I reached the following conclusions. In a general way, one can have an opinion only of that of which one has no knowledge; this is of course a point where we are bound to come across Plato's critique of *doxa*, but it must be added that this lack of knowledge is not self-evident or self-admitted. We can see this in the opinion we can have of a person or a work of art. If I am asked for my opinion of Mozart or Wagner, I am at a loss for an answer. It is as though my experience of Mozart or Wagner were too rich or too intimate, as if I lived with their works in a genuine familiarity. One might say the same of a near kinsman, someone whom I have known for a long time and to whom I am linked by a very strait bond of affection. It seemed to me that opinion can be formed only at a distance; one might say that it is essentially long-sighted, though to use that optical metaphor may be misleading: a long-sighted person sees distant objects more distinctly, whereas it is precisely distinct vision that opinion lacks. Opinion wavers between the two extremes of impression pure and simple, and affirmation. To have an impression of something or someone, is not yet to have a true opinion. Opinion properly so called seems always to imply a '*I maintain that*'. We must note on the one hand that to maintain an opinion is necessarily to maintain it *against* someone else—

the someone may be myself—in so far as I can picture to myself an interlocutor or even an opponent. Such was the discussion I had with myself, which I quoted above. On the other hand, to *maintain* merges imperceptibly with to *claim*. We arrive, then at this definition: in a general way opinion is a *seeming which tends to become a claiming*. And in what does the mechanism of this change consist? That is easily answered; the change comes by lack of reflection. The truth is that if the initial seeming could be recognized as such, as no more than seeming, it could never make way for an affirmation; or, to put it more accurately, the affirmation could be concerned only with the seeming itself. So long, however, as I confine myself to saying that it seems to me that such a person has or lacks such a quality, I stay on *this side* of what is properly called opinion.

These remarks throw a very harsh light on political opinions, for example; it is only too clear that at the root of these opinions there is frequently—I am tempted to say always— nothing but a completely vague *seeming*. But in such matters the development of the *claim* is generally most markedly aggressive. One might even say that the less authentic information there is about the subject under discussion, the more pronounced is that character of aggression; nor would it be extravagant to say that the more information one has on a political matter, the more impossible it is to form a unilateral judgment of it— and opinion is, by definition, unilateral.

So far I have been speaking as though in this matter we were dealing with isolated individualities. The truth, it is only too clear, is very different. As far as political opinions at least are concerned, we know too well that everyone tends simply to reflect what he reads in his morning paper. So it is that we get an imperceptible transition from '*For my part I maintain that*' to '*Everybody knows that*'—and 'everybody knows' actually means 'my paper says'. You can say—and this is particularly true of extremists—that for the man in the street 'my paper' is something that can no more be transcended than can 'my consciousness' for the idealist. Applied to political matters, 'my paper is my consciousness' would hardly be an exaggeration. You might object that it was I, after all, who chose the paper, and it should, accordingly, answer some vague need in my nature which it satisfies. The root of this vague need would lie in my own personal way of valuation. Such an objection is not completely false, but it is none the less far from corresponding to reality. The part played by choice, in this as in other matters, is actually very restricted. The truth is rather that the individual is *submerged* by his surroundings, and in the great majority of instances, what takes place is either imitation properly so called, or a mental contradiction which is simply an inverted form of imitation. You can see this particularly clearly in young middle-class communists who always make a point of contradicting their families and maintain the exact opposite of whatever they accept without question.

To be quite accurate we should, however, distinguish at this point between the essentially impure opinion with which we have been concerned, and an element of ideal justification which corresponds to the more or less inarticulate affirmation of certain values. These values sometimes refer to order and tradition, sometimes to justice and humanity: what I call the *hyperdoxal* element of opinion, the element which cannot be reduced to *doxa* in Plato's meaning.

These considerations give us a base from which to examine

what are called opinions in religious matters. The aspect of claim which I emphasized above is seen nowhere more clearly than in the militant atheist. The atheist is nearly always someone who could express his meaning by saying '*For my part I maintain* that God does not exist'. The tone of defiance is sometimes quite overt—the anarchist atheist, for example, who made a great impression, I suppose, at public meetings by proclaiming, 'God does not exist' and adding, 'If he did, he would strike me dead. I can deny his existence and he does not strike. Therefore he does not exist'. It is evident that the case is the same as the one we looked at before—*I* is taken as *one* or as *everyone*. The atheist more or less explicitly claims that his own opinion or statement is generally held. But if we disregard that claim, what direct experience do we find that he has? In fact it would be more accurate to say that there is no experience, and that its absence is moreover self-evident. I remember a man I knew in a high academic position; what was more, he was a philosopher, or at any rate he appeared in reference books under that description. He once said to me in a debate that if God existed, he would have been made aware of His existence; in other words it was inconceivable that God should be hidden to an eye so penetrating as his. Let us say that he deemed himself too prominent a personality for God not to have introduced Himself to him.

Another thing; we know that the atheist claims to have made good a collection of facts, and that these facts are incompatible with the existence of God. All these facts are connected with the presence of evil in the world. But what then comes in as the factor that determines his position is not so much his actual experience of evil—believers, also have experienced evil in all its manifestations—as a judgment of absolute incompatibility. The atheist's opinion, accordingly, puts itself forward as resting on a rational basis. But it would be well to have a close look at this judgment of incompatibility, and in doing so I shall have to re-open my earlier analysis.

When I am speaking of a particular person and say, 'If that person had been there, such a thing would not have happened; if it happened, it must be because that person was not there', my ground for so speaking is a precise knowledge, or my claim to a precise knowledge, of the person in question. Nurse would have stopped the child from playing with the matches; which means, that she is prudent and careful, she can be trusted completely; she could not have let the child play with matches. But two suppositions are implied in this: first, that the person—the nurse in this case—does really exist; and secondly, that we know her so well that we can say what sort of person she is and what she would do in any given circumstances. The atheist, however, relies not on an experience but on an idea, or pseudo-idea, of God: if God existed, He would have such and such characteristics; but if He had those characteristics He could not allow etc. His judgment of incompatibility, in fact, is based on a judgment of implications. Or rather, what he wants to say is that if the word 'God' has any meaning—of which, indeed, we cannot be certain—it can be applied only to a being who is both completely good and completely powerful. This part of the argument might well be granted; but not so with what follows. When I am speaking of the nurse, I am relying on situations or circumstances which actually occurred, and in which she effectively demonstrated her prudence; or at least on an inner certainty of what I should have done in her place. But does such an assertion retain any meaning when it is applied to the behaviour of

God? Whether those last words have any meaning at all and whether the idea of divine behaviour is not self-contradictory, is a very serious question, but we can leave that on one side for the moment. If I proceed to draw conclusions from what the divine behaviour has been in any particular historical instance, then I am *ipso facto* debarred from agreeing with what the atheist maintains. But is the alternative any better? Can I so put myself in the place of God as to be able to say how I should have behaved in any particular circumstances, what I should have allowed and what I should have forbidden? We may note that when we are speaking of an important public figure who is called upon to make a crucial decision, we often find it impossible to imagine ourselves in his place; in fact the very idea of doing so seems ridiculous. If we pursue that line of thought, we are obliged to recognize the absurdity of trying to put ourselves in God's place. It may be objected, of course, that the statesman has to grapple with a situation which is not of his making, though he has to disentangle it, master it and finally find a solution. But should not God, if He is thought of as a creator, be conceived as having the privilege of needing only to exercise His will? The atheist will say that, if He does not will good, it must be because He Himself does not exist. The extreme insecurity of this position is now very apparent to us, and later it will become progressively more clear that the affirmation of God cannot be separated from the existence of free beings who have reason to think of themselves as creatures. In these circumstances, or at least from one point of view— metaphysically speaking, it may not be a final one, but in the complicated pattern of human life we cannot overlook it— we have grounds for admitting that God Himself may have to to take into account (it would be ridiculous to use the word 'suffer'), in the very name of his creative intention, a state of affairs—an extraordinarily complex pattern, that is, of situations for which men have the right to hold themselves responsible. From this point of view the comparison between God and the statesman in whose place we cannot put ourselves, is not fundamentally as absurd as it seemed at first. This is rather an exoteric way of envisaging the relation between God and the finite beings which He has created free, and I do not claim that it is metaphysically satisfactory. It is only a halting place, and for the moment we may have to leave it behind. But, whatever happens, we cannot just rush by this halt, as an express rushes through a station at which it is not stopping. Let us put it another way, and say that though objections may be raised to the notion of something being *permitted by God*, permitted without being willed, yet it is a notion that cannot just be neglected. It provides a sort of resting place on a certain road; again it provides a way, rather a negative way, no doubt, of rejecting another much cruder conception of the relation between the divine will and the history of mankind.

That digression was necessary, but we must come back to the distinction between opinion and faith which has not yet been completely cleared up. And first it is interesting to note that midway between the two lies the notion of conviction.

Conviction, the fact of *being convinced that*, appears with the character, which may or may not be deceptive, of taking up a definitive position. If I profess republican convictions, I shall assert that I have come to the conclusion, once and for all, that the republican régime is preferable to all others. We may note for a start that my affirmation does not relate only to the immutability of my interior disposition, but by a sort of extension it tends to turn itself into a judgment, arbitrary or

not, which bears upon the object itself. If I really am a convinced republican, in the fullest sense of the word, I shall be
led—arbitrarily, maybe—to assert that the republic will
always meet the requirements of the most reasonable minds.

But on reflection I am obliged to question the legitimacy of
the emphasis on the aspect of finality, in the English sense of
the word. If the term 'unshakeable' is applied to the assertion
of a conviction, does it not always imply a claim which strict
thought can hardly allow? If I were on my guard against a
temptation which has a distinct admixture of pride, the furthest
I could go would be to say: given the constellation which is
made up by my present interior dispositions and the trend of
the events which are known to me at this moment, *I am
inclined to think* that—but it is not apparent by what right I
could affirm the immutability of the constellation itself.

In the political order the unforeseen plays a very large part,
and it is there, accordingly, that all this can be seen most
clearly. Those who have lived right through the fifty years
that have passed since the end of the last century, have only
too solid grounds for appreciating that, at least if their minds
are not distorted by fanaticism—and fanaticism itself is
something of which I shall have more to say.

The point which matters at this stage is the discovery of the
difference in orientation—in polarization, I am almost tempted
to say—between conviction and faith. When a man says that
he is convinced, he puts up a sort of barrier. He claims the
assurance that nothing which may happen later will modify his
way of thinking. Faith, so long as it is conceived in its truth,
has a very different aspect. I should be inclined to say that
when we weigh the matter, we shall have to avail ourselves
again of Bergson's distinction, in his *Les deux Sources de la*

76

Morale et de la Religion, between the open and the closed.

One thing is certain: we must beware of a certain confusion which is embodied in current speech. The verb *to believe* is commonly used in an extremely vague and fluctuating way. It can simply mean, 'I presume' or 'it seems to me'. In that context *to believe* appears as something much weaker and more uncertain than to be convinced. But in our domain, if we are to reach a greater precision of thought, we shall have to concentrate our attention not on the fact of *believing that* but on that of *believing in*. The idea of *credit* can put us on the right lines. We speak of ' opening a credit '; and there, I think, we have an operation which constitutes belief as such. We must not, of course, let ourselves be hypnotized by the material aspect of this operation in the business or financial world. When a bank grants a credit to an individual, it puts at his disposal a certain sum of money, in the hope that this sum will be repaid, with interest, by a predetermined date. It is further agreed between the bank and the individual, that if the sum is not repaid in accordance with the agreement, the bank shall have the right to take certain action against the defaulter.

But as soon as we are concerned with speaking of belief in its proper meaning, we have to get rid of the material ballast, if I may call it such, in this opening of a credit. If I believe in something, it means that I place myself at the disposal of something, or again that I pledge myself fundamentally, and this pledge affects not only *what I have* but also *what I am*. In a modern philosophical vocabulary, this could be expressed by saying that to belief is attached an existential index which, in principle, is completely lacking to conviction. Even if my conviction concerned the nature or worth or merits of a certain person, one would certainly be wrong in saying that, in as much as it was a conviction, it implied on my part anything resembling a pledge to that person. It would, at root, be just as if I lived a sort of self-enclosed existence, and without coming out of my enclosure, I were to pronounce a certain judgment, which did not pledge me to anything. Again, we might put it that from this point of view *to believe* is essentially *to follow*; but we must not attach a passive meaning to that word. The metaphor of *rallying* may very profitably be used to fill out that of credit. If I *believe in*, I *rally to*; with that sort of interior gathering of oneself which the act of rallying implies. From this point of view one might say that the strongest belief, or more exactly the most living belief, is that which absorbs most fully all the powers of your being. Before we go any further, we may note that it will always, admittedly, be possible to translate this belief into the language of conviction. But this translation, I think, will be effected in so far as I am led to discuss my belief with another person; we already know, besides, that this other person may be simply one's own interior interlocutor. To the extent to which I am concerned to account for my belief, I am obliged to treat it as a conviction. That sentence encloses a point of very great importance; because it puts in its right place the idea that a belief is something different from a conviction. The truth is quite certainly much more subtle: it is a question of two completely different vistas — in a certain sense they are even opposite vistas — on something which in so far as it is a content, can in truth be treated as one and the same.

To put it more precisely: if I believe in God and I am questioned or I question myself about this belief, I shall not be able to avoid the assertion that I am convinced of the existence of God. On the other hand, this translation, which is in itself inevitable, misses, I think, what is essential in the belief and is precisely its existential character.

When I spoke of the act of believing *in* . . . I purposely left a blank. But I think we can now fill it in. What can we say of this *X* for whom we open a credit, to whom we rally? We can say, I think, that it is always a reality, whether personal or supra-personal. I may add, moreover, that it is not certain that there is any real opposition between the personal and the supra-personal. I should be much more inclined to admit that the personal is authentically itself only by reason of whatever is in it which smashes the frame in which it is always in danger of allowing itself to be imprisoned as *ego* pure and simple. In any case, I shall be able to open a credit only to what presents itself to me as incapable of being reduced to the condition which is that of *things*. The distinguishing mark of things lies, in fact, in being unable ever to provide me with anything which can be made to resemble an answer. To believe in someone, on the contrary, to place confidence in him, is to say: 'I am sure that you will not betray (*'que tu ne trahiras pas'*) my hope, that you will respond to it, that you will fulfil it'. I have purposely used the second person singular— one cannot have confidence except in a *'toi'*, in a reality which is capable of functioning as *'toi'*, of being invoked, of being something to which one can have recourse. But it is abundantly clear that the assurance which we have just presupposed, is by no means a conviction; it goes beyond what has strictly speaking been given to me, it is a jump, a bet—and, like all bets, it can be lost.

From the sum of these analyses it emerges that I can myself

G   79

be cut off from my own faith and no longer see it; it can even happen that I may come to look on it as an opinion which I have picked up and blindly adopted. But this corresponds to a sort of fall, or to what at any rate a believer has grounds to look upon as a temptation. If the phrase 'to lose one's faith' has any meaning, it designates the position of a being who has fallen in this way and cannot recover himself. We may note also that there is a certain ambiguity in this position. It may happen that the man who has 'lost his faith' looks on himself purely and simply as having been freed from an error and congratulates with himself on this freedom; but it may also be that he feels regret at no longer being in a certain state of blessedness. Even that is an over-simplification of a much more complicated position, for it may be that these two contradict-ory dispositions are co-existent. It is possible, existentially, to admit at times that the state which has been upset correspon-ded to an error and yet to be sorry that one has left it: for when I believed or believed that I believed, I was convinced after all of having the truth; yet there are times when I am so confused that it is possible to go so far as to say, 'After all, can I be sure that then I was mistaken and that now I have the truth?'

If we keep to this outlook, however, we are obliged to grant that it is very difficult, perhaps even impossible, to bridge the gap between the two positions of the man who believes, and the man who does not, or has ceased to, believe. But we must now distinguish between belief taken in its full or comprehensive reality and a particular belief which may always lie open to the attack of primary reflection. So we come back to the problem of confidence properly so-called.

Let us look at an extreme case taken from ordinary daily

life. A banker has approached me, and I have decided to entrust him with a certain sum of money. A friend of mine, however, thinks that he should warn me that there are some ugly rumours about the banker; he has had to leave the town in which he used to live, after an affair that was never properly cleared up. I won't listen to him, I like the banker and I say that I am sure he is the victim of calumnies spread by a competitor of his. I entrust my money to the banker, but the upshot soon shows that my friend was right and that I was dealing with a crook. It is quite likely that the advantageous nature of the banker's proposals helped to deceive me as to his own character. This is a case on which critical reflection could work freely. But we can imagine a very different case. Take a mother who refuses to despair of her son, in spite of the deceptions he has practised on her and the deliberate lies he has often told her; she still refuses to listen to the advice of those who tell her to wash her hands of her unworthy son, or at least not to give him the money for which he asks her. What is the difference, not simply the psychological, but the strictly metaphysical, difference, between the two situations? Everything goes to show that it concerns the actual nature of the intersubjective bond. In the first case we may say that such a bond does not exist, by which I mean that there is no relation between one being and another being. The banker is not my friend, even if I am taken in by his prepossessing bearing and his charming ways and feel something like sympathy with him. One might say that in this case the banker comes in only as a tempter, rather like an advertisement which raises boundless hopes in simple minds. In the other case the converse is true. There will doubtless be people to say to the mother, 'You refuse to see your son in his true light, you persist in seeing him as you would like him to be'. But even if this objection seems well grounded at first, it implies a misunderstanding of a fundamental datum—that the mother, in as much as she is a mother, is incapable of forming an objective picture of her son; she may even be quite without the right to do so, if we admit—and it is after all strictly true—that gestation is protracted well beyond birth properly so called, such birth being, spiritually speaking, only a pre-birth. It would be a mistake, however, not to go further here than the fact of gestation taken in its literal sense. It is more a question of a taking in charge, and that is what is effected in all love worthy of the name. It seems, however, that this taking in charge should not be understood strictly as a voluntary commitment; let us keep in mind that in this case the voluntary act is settled on an affirmation of a different order, and that that order is properly speaking ontological. I say 'an affirmation'—I should not acknowledge that I have the right to speak in this instance of intuition. Present-day philosophers who have used that word have, I think, been too much inclined to lose sight of the fact that intuition is a viewing, the derivation of the word is optical. Here, it seems, nothing like this can be in question. We are faced by an assurance which in many respects may be defined as an anticipation of something which, discursively, could be reached only by successive stages. We might describe it, as we did before, by the metaphor of a short cut across the zigzags of a mountain track. There is no doubt that to critical reflection such an assurance can appear only as a pretension without anything in it to justify itself; but it is precisely the conditions under which this assurance can be anything but pretension that we now have to discover.

I have said elsewhere that pretension is always essentially

centred on the *I*, the *I* who make the claim. It is not enough to say that the pretension is the expression of the *I*; in reality it *constitutes* it. It would be absurd, moreover, to deny that confusion can arise between the domain of pretension and that of love; but it arises only as love fails, and the nature of this failure is just what we have to put our finger on. A wife, for example, might well say to her mother-in-law, in a markedly aggressive tone, 'I can claim to know my husband as well as you do, if not better'; but that remark implies that an element of what is really rivalry, or, if you like, a competitive element, is introduced. One could say that the young woman claims to base her remark on experience that she has acquired, on an 'I have always noticed'. She is speaking as an expert, as a specialist addressing laymen. That, however, is precisely the attitude that a being who is animated by a true love will never adopt, or will at least reproach itself immediately for adopting; for such an attitude fundamentally cannot but be degrading to the person to whom it is directed; indirectly, too, to the person who adopts it. Taken to extremes, it practically amounts to denying the liberty and uniqueness of the loved being; for at bottom it amounts to putting him in a category and labelling him.

The degradation for the person himself who adopts the attitude lies in that the specialist as such ceases to behave as one being open to another being; to benefit a technique he betrays intersubjective reality.

But can we rise to a clearer and more positive view of what constitutes the non-pretension which lies at the root of the assurance of which I spoke? One word will prove helpful; true love is humble. Now, it is precisely the positive notion of humility which tends to become unintelligible to beings who

are imbued with belief in the value of technique. This brings
us to one of the critical points of our enquiry; and we shall have
to concern ourselves with its examination in my next chapter.

CHAPTER VI

PRAYER AND HUMILITY

IN a general way it would seem that thinkers, so far as they concentrated their attention on humility, have contented themselves with looking at it from a point of view which is either psychological or ethico-theological. But if we are to follow up the line of our enquiry, it is the metaphysical outlook which concerns us most. If humility is conceived as Sartre, for instance, conceives it, it can only be emphatically denied: or, to put it more exactly, it can only be robbed of its value in the name of existential psychoanalysis. The tendency will be to see in it only a sadistic craving for mortification. In this instance, as always with the author of *L'Être et le Néant*, the analysis holds good only in a quite restricted area of the life of consciousness ; to put it more exactly, of a life of degraded consciousness. And it is in taking an arbitrary and sophistic step that the philosopher extends to other sectors the conclusions he has reached in this one.

There is room, no doubt, for a pathology of humility, or, more exactly, of humiliation. There are striking examples of it in Dostoievsky. But humility is not a taste for self-humiliation. We could go so far as to say that it consists not in the act of self-humiliation, but rather in the recognition of our own nothingness. At the root of humility lies the more or less unexpressed assertion, 'By myself, I am nothing and I can do nothing except in so far as I am not only helped but premoted in my being by Him who is everything and is all-powerful'.

It may be objected that this is an arbitrary interpretation, in as much as it ties humility up with categories of a specifically religious order; but the truth would seem to be that the difference between humility and modesty lies precisely in this, that the latter, and the latter only, can be just a natural or profane *habitus*, whereas humility properly so called presupposes a certain affirmation of the sacred. It is by that affirmation that humility is in the most radical opposition to *hybris*, which one may describe as essentially sacrilegious. We may note, too, that sacrilege depends in a way upon the sacred in order to deny it, or rather to defy it, and that in that sense a philosopher of *hybris* who categorically denies the sacred cuts the ground from under his own feet. That, again, can be seen very clearly in Sartre: if his atheism is not to sink to the level of sheer platitude, it needs a god as a target for his denial. It is, after all, to use a distinction to which I attach importance, and to which I alluded previously, an *anti-theism* rather than an *a-theism*. Numerous riders could be developed from this point, notably on the subject of the incompatibility of humility and technique, in so far as the latter claims to function over the whole range of human activities: in other words, in so far as it tends to become technocracy or technomania. There is no doubt at all that an engineer can be humble, but he can be humble only in so far as he keeps something in reserve beyond the world of theoretical and applied calculations which is his own professional world.

This may be an appropriate place at which to consider whether there is or is not an identity of nature between humility, properly so called, and that effacement of self which is implied by every objective knowledge. Reflection would seem to answer in the negative. The effacement of self actually consists purely and simply in abstracting from a certain number of recognized contingent conditions. But humility properly so called is of quite a different order; it is a mode of being, far removed from amounting to a collection of methodological precautions. The scientist has to guarantee his work against a whole series of possible errors which up to a point can be gauged in advance. Once he has taken these precautions he has both the power and even the duty to be emphatic in his assertions. But humility has nothing at all in common with this concern to rule out error; in the case of humility it is not error that is to be feared, but rather a claim which is incompatible with our condition of finite beings, the claim which would consist in believing that we are, or have the power to make ourselves, dependent only upon ourselves. The question arises only so soon as I take cognizance of my quality as a subject and of its hidden implications. But for the scientist as such this quality can never be included in his reckoning; in that, moreover, lies the nobility of his vocation. The work to which, within the limits of his specialization, he has to devote himself, enforces a realist attitude; but there is no abuse until he tries to claim a metaphysical justification for that attitude.

We may note on the other hand that with many of our contemporaries a pride which is essentially like that of Prometheus has become almost an habitual disposition, and they will accordingly show, in spite of everything, a marked propensity to confuse humility and humiliation. By that I mean calling humiliating, and hence injustifiable, the act by which a human consciousness is led to acknowledge itself as tributary to something other than itself. I may remind the reader that this acknowledgment is always liable to degenerate according as the other-than-self is levelled down to the stage of something inferior to the individual consciousness; if it sinks, that is to say, to a sociological reality which has never, in fact, and never will become genuinely conscious of itself. The world today shows us terrifying examples of what this moral masochism can become. I am thinking primarily, of course, of the self-condemnation pronounced in the course of a large number of trials staged in countries of Eastern Europe by men who declared that they had deserved all the penalties which their judges had decided to inflict on them. The word 'judge', I may add, should not be used here: judgment does not come into the matter at all; it is rather some sort of transposition into a pseudo-juridical plane of ritual actions as practised among so-called primitive peoples. It is in fact a make-believe. Nor must it be held that this self-condemnation is obtained in every case by the administration of drugs or the cutting of certain nerves. There are techniques—so-called psychological techniques—which can be effective enough by themselves. Moreover, instances are known in which the subject has been left entirely by himself, without any visible restraint, and has ended by developing a complex of guilt, which has led him to make the desired admissions of his own accord. Here we are at the very heart of ignominy, precisely because consciousness abdicates in favour of what we should call a pseudo- or an infra-consciousness. There is no common measure shared by such a situation and that in which the human creature turns humbly and freely towards Him from Whom it holds its very being. But we must realize at the same time that the opposition between the two is fated to be more and more misunderstood in such a time as ours. In our time society, in its most restrictive form, is either literally divinized in the totalitarian states and those threatened by totalitarianism; or develops the tendency (and some theologians are partly to blame for this) to make for itself a degraded image of God, of the divine power, which a true believer would be the first to consider offensive.

Our enquiries last year gave us a clear warning against this image; for they brought to light what I designated by the name of *creative receptivity* : a thing which, with very few exceptions, has been so strangely misunderstood by idealist philosophies. Sartre, however strongly he may claim to be the philosopher of the 'project', of the *se faire*, is still, whether he admits it or not, the heir of these philosophies; but it should be added that the greatest representatives of idealism—Fichte I am thinking of particularly—retained an extraordinarily vigorous realization of values; and it must be added further, that the *absolute I* which is the starting point of the *Wissenschafts-lehre* has certainly nothing in common with the projecting subject of *L'Être et le Néant*. What we are bound to notice here, there can be no doubt, is a phenomenon of degeneration.

These have been only apparent digressions; it is, in fact, only by working in a roundabout way that we can state in their specific reality the fundamental notions at which we are aiming.

To carry further what I said above, I should say that the more it is an authentically transcendent reality which is effectively revered, the more it holds a warning for the being which turns its dazzled eyes to it, not to be tempted into what would properly be called debasing itself before reality. Another way of putting this would be to say that in so far as there is such a thing as religious masochism, it is always a perversion. The words 'authentic transcendence' will need interpretation; and, as we have so often found before, we shall have to reach that interpretation by an indirect approach. It is quite obvious as soon as we think of the false prophets we have seen swarming around us. When I speak of 'false prophets' I am not thinking only of their often having been wrong in their predictions, or of their bragging about powers which are not theirs. There is no doubt that they have exercised a really magical ascendancy over a large number of men who have either heard them directly or have been exposed to their propaganda in some other way. However little we may be masters of certain sectarian dispositions which can exist in any of us, what gives us legitimate grounds for calling them false prophets is this: that they have all claimed to announce, even to set up, a particular order, and this while they aggressively mis-understand the conditions without which no true order at all can be founded. On this point it is of prime importance to rejoin the path marked out by the highest philosophic thought since Socrates and Plato on the one hand, and the highest reli-gious preaching on the other; we have the right, and even the obligation, without falling into a rash syncretism, to keep in mind the implications of certain revealing points of agree-ment between the higher religions. Every prophet who denies the universal should be looked on as a false prophet. That is only a preliminary indication; later on we shall have to ask ourselves more precisely at what sort of universality we are aiming; we know too well how this notion of the concrete universal has degenerated with the descendants of Hegelianism, and even perhaps, after all, with the Hegel of the last period.

The preliminary conclusion, then, at which we are arriving, and it is an important one, is that at all costs a connection must be maintained between authentic transcendence and true universality, and that without this mankind inevitably falls into idolatry.

It must be granted that this assertion itself could always be questioned in the name of a certain *a priori*. Nietzsche comes to mind as an obvious example—I am thinking, of course, of the Nietzsche of the last period, and not of the intermediate period, the period of *Menschliches, allzu Menschliches*, or of *Morgenröthe*. For Nietzsche, transcendence is a going beyond, and the word has a more precise meaning here than it has with most of our contemporaries, man being obliged to rise above himself by an heroic effort, not perhaps in order to become the superman, but to make way for him. It is obvious that in Nietzsche's eyes the superman will trample on all the principles which hold good for the common man, that is to say for the ordinary man; and that idea has given birth to a great deal of nonsense. There is no doubt at all that Nietzsche never granted for a second that the Superman could allow himself a licence which would be denied to ordinary men. If he has·to show hardness, it is above all because he is hard to himself, and that in the most extreme degree. One might say that for Nietszche the Superman has to face the utmost difficulty and danger; and that from a certain point of view the concept should be retained even though the idea of the advent of the Superman should be looked on as mythological, even—for in spite of everything it is still tied up with a certain evolutionist dogmatism — looked down on as a myth in the worst sense of the word. If one endeavoured to set up what would be a remote transposition of Nietzsche's thought, one might perhaps say the *authentic universal* of which we spoke is as little assimilable as possible to the masses as

91

such: and it is just the mass-man which Nietzsche already rejects. Our own ghastly experience forces us to think that the masses naturally conform with the various sorts of propaganda which are spread nowadays by means of the extraordinarily powerful methods of publicity available; but propaganda itself is the favourite weapon of the false prophets or of those who spread their doctrincs.

We have still, however, failed to get rid of the objections which were put to us. We cannot fail to notice that, at least in certain sectors of contemporary thought, the universal, when it is thus purged, consists in a set of values which are preferred or chosen by some individuals, while others are indifferent to them. This is to stay on the plane of pure subjectivity, that is, fundamentally, of choice in its most gratuitous form.

We must, however, face the fact that if this possibility were to be accepted, it would be the end of man and of the order which in the course of history he has tried, painfully and at the cost of countless experiments, to establish for himself. The way would then lie open to the worst abuses and to abominations which are expressly condemned by the very people who are so incredibly frivolous as to defend this idea of a choice of values. Significant, too, is the sort of sneering contempt which some of these philosophers are inclined to show for moral traditions which have for so long been recognized as sacred. By a most unhappy confusion, they will sometimes go so far, particularly in the domain of sex, as to label as pharisaical all conduct that we call virtuous, without making any distinction between prejudice and the free adoption of loose conduct.

At the same time, is there not a danger, when we speak of rules freely adopted, that we may find ourselves thrown back below the level on which our enquiries are being carried out, and remaining in the sphere of pure ethics; is there not a risk that in the end we may find ourselves back in a more or less emended Kantian formalism?

There is no doubt that it would be untimely and even highly imprudent in these days to depreciate Kantian ethics. By asserting once and for all that persons should be treated as ends in themselves, Kant has anticipated us in his just and definitive condemnation of the shocking practices which we have seen multiply before our eyes, and there is indeed a sense in which it is to this assertion that we are continually compelled to return. But at the same time it must be added that if the Kantian formula held a privileged position, notably with many free-thinkers of the late nineteenth century, it was because they enjoyed without knowing it a mental climate soaked in the Christian spirit: this our contemporaries have lost. Kant's delusion probably lay in thinking that there was no reason to take this mental climate into account; that reason, in fact, could legislate without considering the historical context in which moral subjects have to act under concrete conditions. This omission would seem to be legitimate only in the domain of abstract relations, particularly in mathematics; but I think that in these days we must recognize that it does not hold good in the same way when we are concerned with what Kant called persons, and that his mistake lay, no doubt, in looking at the matter outside any existential perspective. What I want to stress, moreover, is not at all that it may be possible to introduce at this point a relativism which would eventually tend to annul, to annihilate the affirmations of the moral conscience, but rather that the qualities proper to those affirmations and the way in which they should actually be considered, cannot be taken as being independent of the concrete context which is their setting.

This digression has not been without a purpose. Our aim is to allow ourselves a more precise view of the nature of the venerable (*le réveréntiel*) which must be posited if humility is to be true and significant. Here again it is important to refer to Kant; it would not be easy nowadays to agree with the view of respect which he gave in his *Critique of Practical Reason*, but that by no means implies that his view is mistaken. It would be more accurate, I think, to express the truth as follows: it is as though there were a general change of perspective, and in this change the same reality shows us a different contour—as a mountain massif does, when we shift our ground. I should go so far as to suggest, for example, that since Kant's time the notions of *Gesetz* and *Gesetzmässigkeit* have lost much of their prestige, and that this is perhaps partly because they are now embodied in a system of state-regulations whose arbitrary and murderous character is daily more woefully felt by serious thinkers.

This may give rise, it is true, to a mistaken interpretation which I mention only *in order to rule it out*. I have spoken of a shifting of perspective, but it would be extremely dangerous to think of that shift as a progress, in the sense of the word which has prevailed since the philosophers of the latter half of the eighteenth century. I shall certainly have to expound my own views on this notion in my last chapter; it is one which seems to me to be at present applicable exclusively to the technical sphere, but at this point I shall say that we must do no more than state this shifting of perspective, without giving an opinion as to the label we should attach to it.

Now that we have done something to clear the ground, we

can begin to consider how the pure *révérentiel* should appear to us. And it is now that we must persevere in our efforts to guard against prematurely formulating conclusions which derive from current theological thought.

Here we meet the paradox that while religion implies distance, yet as distance tends to be annihilated, religion is degraded. The English word *worship* seems to fit the case particularly well. At this point we have to take into account a tendency which is very common among our contemporaries; it consists in bringing out the purely subjective character of religion and is only apparently counterbalanced by a concentration on the so-called sociological aspects of this 'phenomenon'. Our minds have been so shaped, or mis-shapen, by idealism that it is only with the greatest difficulty that we can refrain from locating in the subject, which is reduced to its mere psychological function, not the attributes but rather, let us say, the energies with which the adorer endows the reality he adores. There you have an extension or a simple expression of the revolution, as fundamental as that of Copernicus, whose fulfilment in his own time was Kant's main achievement. It is true that the sociologist claims to free himself from the fetters of subjectivism by asserting that adoration is not the act of an isolated consciousness but rather of a constituted group. But the answer to this is that Kierkegaard's protest is still unanswerable in itself, without at the same time being of such a nature as to make us overlook the presence of a genuinely collective element in religious life. Even if I pray alone in my room, we can and should maintain that I am uniting myself by or in this prayer to a community which does not belong exclusively, or even primarily, to the visible world. But this bears little relation to the claims of an objective sociology which concentrates on the institutional aspect of religious life.

We have reached a point at which we must note that prayer is not brought in as in any way a contingent fact; on the contrary it is the essential datum, although we have in reality no right to make any categorical pronouncement about the forms that it must take, and we must certainly beware of a formalism which grants validity only to certain specific prayers. If we reflect on this, we shall have to ask precisely what meaning the notion of validity can bear in this context. Without going so far as to say that in such a domain it is purely and simply inadequate, we should at least resolutely rule out the idea of a sort of official stamp which can be put on or withheld from any particular prayer. We must emphasize, moreover, that visas and permits have been given an extravagant importance in the world today, and it would be intolerable to attempt to force them in any way into the realm on which we are now focussing our attention. We can only guess that some prayers may be more pure than others, and some may be completely impure. I should be inclined to think that these ideas of purity and non-purity ought to be substituted for those of validity and non-validity. But what actually is this purity? Should we interpret it as a conformity with essence? In that case, what is this essence of prayer? What is it that allows us to say that one prayer is more authentically prayer than another?

Let us look at a petition or request as such, and, more precisely, the petition as centred on itself. For example, I can pray that a disease from which I am suffering may be cured. There is no doubt that it would be unjust to say that such a prayer is not legitimate, although it must be granted that it is not without some kinship with purely human requests addressed to other beings who are themselves also purely human. In other words, it seems that in my prayer I imply the existence of a powerful being, even an all-powerful being, on whom my cure depends in the same way, for example, as a prisoner's release depends on a tyrant. One might perhaps think that if this request is impure, it is because it implies an assimilation which tends to reduce God to a non-divine scale. What at first seems strange is that when the request refers not to me but to someone else, even though it may be a very near kinsman, we cannot but think of it as less impure than the first sort of request; and yet in this case the assimilation of which I spoke is even more obviously presupposed. But reflection will show us clearly that if I have in me a capacity for prayer, I have not, strictly speaking, the right not to appeal to this mysterious power on behalf of another, from the moment when I realize, however vaguely, that I am responsible for what concerns him. To refuse to pray for him would be to forsake and betray him; and we should perhaps add that, if my faith is real, it is impossible for me not to think that the being whom I invoke will take into account the act by which I assume this responsibility.

The situation is complicated by a mixture of elements; what I mean is, that as I am in a way carnally attached to the being for whom I am praying, my prayer could always be looked upon as somewhat selfish. But I do not think that I have the right to give way to a sort of excessive purism, and argue from the relative impurity of my prayer that I have no right to pray for the safety of the person who is in danger. It may well be understood that the idea of God implied in that case is nevertheless already much more pure than that implied in the purely selfish request; what we now presuppose is the active recognition, in God and through God, of the bond which constitutes all real love.

It is true that a further question, complementary to the first, might well be put at this point: under what conditions can love be known as genuine? At this stage of our investigation we may be satisfied with saying that my love is the more authentic according as I love less for my own sake, that is for what I can hope to obtain from another, and more for the sake of the other. That is, however, only a cut and dried answer, and still implies too dualist a notion of the lover and the loved. Will not the truth be found to lie rather in the more and more indivisible community, in the bosom of which I and the other tend to be continually more perfectly absorbed? So one might come to distinguish, taking the act itself of praying as a starting point, the possibility of a progress in the actual way in which God is thought of. We must grant, however, that to do so is bound to give rise to objections. The first would be that we may be arbitrary in asserting as a principle that the selfish request is spiritually speaking inferior to that which is made on behalf of another. To meet this objection we shall do well to avail ourselves again of secondary reflection; we must, that is, bring out the full implications of the idea by virtue of which it is alleged that such an affirmation may be condemned as arbitrary. Some years before the war I remember hearing one of a small party of guests, a young man evidently of marxist tendencies, say that we do not yet know what are the true values, and that we must wait for science to progress further and enlighten us. The fact is, however, that such a notion testifies to a lack of reflection that is really distressing. How can one imagine for a moment that the future development of science will be able to throw any light on true values? All we can anticipate is a continuation of more and more extensive research, from which we shall learn what is judged to be good or bad in different types of society. We can easily imagine also that a sort of social physics might explain approximately the connection, for example, between various moral beliefs and the birth or suicide rate. But it is quite obvious that such conclusions can tell us nothing about values. It is beyond the power of science to tell us whether it is right or wrong to increase the population; it will only be able to remind us that unless certain economic conditions are fulfilled, over-population can become a grave social danger. As for what are called popular polls, they are necessarily without any real significance. It would be ridiculous to suppose that the majority can ever get a clear view of these matters; the contrary is much more true. We may admit that Ibsen's phrase, 'the majority is always wrong' goes too far, but we must realize all the same that in this connection the category of number has no significance at all.

The outcome of all these considerations is the conclusion that whatever technical progress posterity may make when compared with us, there will be no progress in its knowledge of values themselves. I shall go further and say that if there is no sign of conversion—in my last chapter we shall have to consider the nature of this conversion—the technocratic craze will gradually succeed in drowning every feeling for values; and this precisely because they are eternal, and a man who lived two thousand years ago was at bottom no better and no worse off than we are, for knowing what is or is not right.

To go back, however, to where we started: it is literally beside the point to imagine that a more advanced science than our own could one day enable us to assert the primacy of the selfish demand over the demand which is not selfish. In that there would be no progress, only the most terrifying retrogression. Moreover, we must remember that in such a sphere it is not just a question of a simple step backward— there is a danger of falling far below the level at which we started; far below, to be more precise, the level of pre-christian thought, of a thought, that is, which was a preparation, though maybe a distant one, not only for welcoming Revelation, but even for the acceptance of any moral evidence.

This detour, then, has shown us quite clearly wherein lies the legitimacy of judging to be inauthentic a prayer which pivots on *me*, and on *me* alone. But does this give us any ground for saying that the God to whom the prayer is addressed does not exist? Conversely, shall we be right in alleging that it is impossible for the God of the other prayer, of the authentic prayer, not to exist? Before we answer these questions, we must reflect on the use of the words *existence* and *non-existence* when they are meant to apply to a being who cannot form part of the web of our experience.

In such matters, however carefully we may choose our terminology—and this refinement is often misleading—it is still extremely difficult to rule out certain considerations which hold good only in the empiric world. Obviously I can write a letter or address a request to a personage of whom I have heard and who I have been told is all-powerful; but it may well be that this personage does not exist, and in that case my letter will be sent back to me marked 'addressee unknown'. But in this same world it would still be wrong to say that because my letter contained a selfish request, it was bound to come back to me with that post office mark. In other words, in what we call 'our world' there cannot be any suspicion of a sure or guaranteed connection between the content of the request and the existence or non-existence of the person to whom it is addressed. But it is important to be fully aware of the difference between that realm and the one in which we are struggling to make our way. We must keep in mind a point we made before: in this sphere the opposition between far and near is transcended. No sort of transmission, accordingly, can be conceived, for the medium, whatever it may be, in which the transmission should take place is absent.

From now on, we must make a strict rule not to ask ourselves whether *there is* or is not someone in whom we could find certain attributes which would allow us to qualify him as God. But that is not all. It would also be unreasonable to claim, as the atheists claim, that there is no one who has such attributes. And it would be as unreasonable to conceive of the person who prays as addressing himself to someone who receives his prayer —as a tyrant receives a petitioner—as it would be to maintain that the individual who prays does so in the void. The phrase 'in the void' is particularly useful for stimulating reflection. It is enough to think of people who speak in the void—they address themselves to a listener who is either absent or incapable of hearing them.

But how can we hope to overcome this opposition which is valid and meaningful only in the empirical order? The great difficulty with which we are faced seems to me to be this: if I try to reconcile the contradiction, shall I not be inclined to persuade myself that the act of praying, unlike the act of asking, contains in itself its own answer, its own granting, I might say? But is the granting an answer to the need which is implied in the prayer? I think it would be difficult to maintain such a view. Prayer, as we see it practised by the most fervent souls, can in no instance be understood as containing in itself its own granting. On the contrary, it may be thought of as depending on the mysterious will of an incomprehensible power whose plans we cannot fathom. The man who is praying thinks of himself as quite uncertain, however hopeful he may be, of the answer which will be made to his prayer.

Should we, then, say that in as much as the praying consciousness takes heed of its uncertainty, it is labouring under an error or delusion, that to some extent it is misled by an anthropomorphic realism; and add that it is the philosopher's business to expose and denounce this delusion? That would be an extremely dangerous position to take up, I must admit. It amounts to giving primacy to philosophy in matters that concern religious life, and the final result of that is to depreciate the latter. That is what the intellectualist teachings of the past, particularly those derived from Spinoza, have done. The philosophy of existence, as I have tried to define it, cannot but be completely dissatisfied with such a devaluation.

The truth is probably that when prayer is pure—and I need not elaborate again the meaning of purity in this context— it cannot be thought of as remaining unanswered; it cannot be like a letter which the addressee has left unopened or thrown by mistake or without bothering into the waste paper basket. The believer cannot feel sure that he has a living relation with God, without, by reason of that certainty, having grounds for a pronouncement on the manner in which empirically his prayer will be granted. It would seem that what is definitely excluded is the possibility that his prayer may be treated as though it had never been made. This is only to be expected in so far as we do not ourselves take prayer seriously or as our manner of praying is a justification, by way of a salving of our conscience, of this sort of more or less unacknowledged contempt of prayer.

From this again we can see, and this time indirectly, how we are in a position to distinguish what authentic prayer can be. It can be neither the request which we discussed before, nor a mechanical recitation of formulae. We could add that it is nothing if not a certain very humble and fervent way of *uniting oneself with . . .*—though we must admit that that phrase itself is still inadequate. The fact is that in a general way it is almost impossible for us to think of union except in relation to what is akin to us, in which case we integrate ourselves into a whole whose elements are homogeneous. In the case of prayer such a union cannot be thought of. Here the mystery lies in that I have to merge in something which infinitely transcends me, and at first it seems impossible to conceive such a thing. It might perhaps be suggested that the union we claim might be interpreted as a surrender—but a surrender to what? To a will whose ends and whose very nature go infinitely beyond anything we can conceive. But would not that amount to a blind unconditional surrender? 'Whatever you may will, your will shall be mine.'

It is not to be denied that the believer feels that this absolute submission seems to be required of him by the being in whom he has faith, but it would appear extremely difficult to maintain this formula, and for a very simple reason: in the world in which we have, literally, been put, it is extremely difficult for us to distinguish what is willed and what is only permitted. It is quite impossible to imagine that any circumstance at all should be looked on as willed for its own sake, simply because I am faced by that circumstance; otherwise we might end in approving the manifestly absurd attitude of those who think it sacrilegious to treat a disease medically or to cure it by an operation. (Such an attitude, moreover, is unanimously condemned as unreasonable nowadays, except for one or two sects, and one might well go further into the reasons for that condemnation.)

Reflection seems to make it quite clear that we have to force our way between two errors which are of very different natures, and the path is narrow and full of obstacles. One of the errors lies in taking up a position exclusively within the sphere of causality, which is to say of technique. From that point of view, prayer would appear as a pure epiphenomenon, or rather as auto-suggestion. The other error, which I pointed out just above, lies on the contrary in neglecting, that is to say, in dismissing as non-existent, the correlations which reason enables us to disclose. The truth would seem to be that we must try to understand how 'the spirit of prayer' can be fitted in with the series of positive steps which reason demands in any given situation. To take a very simple example: we may readily imagine that a surgeon who is a believer may feel the need for prayer before he undertakes a particularly difficult operation. It is by no means impossible to imagine how this prayer may open and clear the road for his action. But the situation with which he has to deal cannot really be thought of *either* as having been willed or produced by the divine will, considered as a pure agent, *or* as being a mere link in a chain of cause and effect —which is what a metaphysic determinist in inspiration would maintain that it is. By this second hypothesis the only way out would be in the direction of a stoicism which would disregard the situation as being quite indifferent in its bearing upon a certain inalienable essence in the subject. Ultimately, however, this is sheer fiction, though it may be a very noble fiction. To take an extreme example, a man suffering from an incurable disease cannot take refuge in this lofty *apatheia*; or, if we can imagine that he might, he will always be liable to entertain doubts of the validity of such an attitude. The truth is rather that he should look at the position as touching him very fundamentally. Can we, then, see how what I have called the spirit of prayer may be manifested in a similar case? Or again, that union of which we said that it could not be reduced to the union which can be achieved between finite beings?

The spirit of prayer, I think, may first be defined negatively as the rejection of a temptation; and the temptation would consist in being shut in on oneself in pride or despair, two things which are closely connected. Positively, however, is not the spirit of prayer seen to be primarily a receptive disposition towards everything which can detach me from myself and from my tendency to blind myself to my own failings? It is not, however, simply a spirit of detachment; the man who is concerned only with abstracting from himself is still but at the beginning of a road which climbs infinitely higher. We may note, moreover, that the progress which is possible is not required by anything resembling a dialectical necessity. It is an unfortunate delusion, fostered by philosophers like Hegel, that belief entails such a necessity. This delusion is tied up, also, with a phenomenon of pure substitution. Simple representations arranged by thought to suit itself, as one might deal out a pack of cards, are substituted for the real phases of a development which is that of the existent. All one can say is that when thought works *a posteriori* on a development which is in reality a conversion (we shall try later to attach a more precise meaning to 'conversion') it is always on the road to interpreting it dialectically. Bergson is here the necessary complement to Kierkegaard.

It would be quite useless, however, to disguise the fact that everything we have said so far is still shrouded in ambiguity. Both the non-believing and the believing philosopher who counts himself obliged to make a provisional abstraction from his personal belief, are inevitably involved in a persistent and almost ineluctable difficulty. When we speak of the spirit of prayer, can we mean anything but an interior disposition? Do we not feel that we are enclosed in a circle in which consciousness seems to come back on itself? Once more secondary reflection has to be called in. To what do we oppose this 'anything but'? Surely it is the idea we rejected earlier of a sort of external relation between the person who prays and the person who should hear his prayer but may be absent? But we must repeat and emphasize what we said above: if prayer is to be recognized as real, it must be possible to mark out a road to serve as an intermediary. Every time, however, that we try to advance along this road we are open to the temptation of putting forward again the dilemma which we have been concerned to circumvent. We must realize from the start that the more we look at the believer from a monadist point of view, the more insoluble and even, no doubt, meaningless, the problem will appear. It is here more than anywhere that we may see the strict connection which links this second series of lectures to the first. Prayer is possible only when intersubjectivity is recognized, where it is operative. We must, it is true, keep well in mind that intersubjectivity can never be looked upon as a mode of structure which can be stated or verified in any way; that would be to make it into a spurious sort of objectivity. The positive corollary of this is that the intersubjective can only be acknowledged freely, and that implies further that it is always within our power to deny it. I can always behave as though I had in reality no means of access to the reality of another, as though the other were only a bunch of possibilities to be made use of, or of threats to be neutralized. There we have a practical solipsism, and this solipsism can not only be overt but even, if I may so put it, can provide its own justification. It is only, however, the man who has contrived to make his way into the intersubjective sphere who can see this practical solipsism as nothing but a blinding, and a blinding which is at least to some extent voluntary. One may, in fact, say almost with certainty that there is nobody who has all his life been so unlucky as to have found it impossible ever to unite himself with another, or obliged to deny the other as a real presence.

In my next chapter, however, we shall have to define more precisely exactly what we should understand in this context by liberty; for there we have an idea, or something more than an idea, which philosophers, and contemporary philosophers in particular, have done their best to obscure.

CHAPTER VII

FREEDOM AND GRACE

IN my last lecture I chiefly tried to disclose certain fundamental connections: in particular we saw that it seems
possible to recognize prayer as real only when intersubjectivity
is found in it; and a Christian will have grounds for thinking
that the fullest experience we can be granted of this is provided by the Church, although that does not mean that anything is specified as to the theological concept we should form
of it. We must realize, too, that intersubjectivity itself cannot
be considered in any way as a structure comparable to that
which comes within the grasp of objective knowledge. Here the
example of the Church can be revealing. If it is impossible
even for the adversaries of the Church to call her existence
into doubt, it is only in as much as she is one institution among
others, that is, at bottom, in as much as she is not the Church;
and from that point of view it will always be permissible for
these same adversaries to see in her nothing but a machine,
built up, for example, by the propertied classes to mystify
and crush those they oppress. If we are to think of it as a
Church, as, that is, an *agape* or as incarnate intersubjectivity,
we must in some way at least be on the inside of it. I say 'in
some way', because even if I am quite unconscious of belonging to the Church, I can have a sort of diviner's sympathy
which detects a mode of intersubjective presence from which
the Church derives her value and significance. Hence it would

appear that I am free, according to the sort of person I am, to deny the Church or on the other hand to recognize her; and so it is just by this circuitous route that we have reached our view of freedom. It is apparent, of course, that freedom was to some extent presupposed, but in a way which was still approximate and vague, by all that has been said since the beginning of this second series; now we must scrutinise with care exactly what we are to understand by freedom or free will. But there is more. It might well be objected that whether the choice of allegiance is real or evoked by sympathy, it depends much less on freedom properly so called than on grace, on a gift, that is, which might have been granted to me or withheld from me. Thus the real problem would now turn on the intimate relation which must be established between gift and freedom, between freedom and grace. Everything will depend on the answer we ultimately give to this most difficult of all questions; whether we shall be able to make up our minds about the very existence of God; or, to put it more accurately, to give definite expression to the type of solution which, in the eyes of a metaphysician, can be given to the general question which has been at the centre of all our enquiries since the beginning of this second series.

If I am to take into account my own living experience, it is apparent that the first question I must ask myself is: up to what point or within what limits can I or can I not assert that I am a free being. I have purposely put the question in the first person, because after all it is a question which can only be asked by me of myself. No outside answer will satisfy me, unless it coincides with my own answer, unless ultimately it *is my answer*.

At the same time it is impossible to overlook the difficulty in which I become involved as soon as I ask myself this question. Can I with all sincerity answer it by a comprehensive 'yes' or 'no'? To begin with, am I quite sure of the meaning which I am to attach to it? It is true that I can interpret it in a way which seems, at any rate, to be simple enough: am I conscious of doing what I want to do? The question would then revolve round the bond which unites will to action. But it is only too clear that there are countless instances in which I by no means do what I want to do; and we have the support of irrefutable evidence when we say that certain beings in captivity, in conditions, that is, which would involve the reduction to a minimum of what we commonly think of as independence, have nevertheless enjoyed a much deeper experience of their inner freedom than they would have been able to do in what we all call normal life. These considerations would lead us to presume that there is a freedom which is not concerned with *doing*; after all, the phrase 'do what I want to do', is at bottom ambiguous. To want, indeed,—I take this word in the sense of the French *vouloir*—is not to desire. The question with which we should now be concerned certainly cannot consist in asking ourselves whether or no I do what I desire. It might well be—the stoics first saw this, and all the subsequent thinkers who drew their inspiration from stoicism— that will is essentially opposed to desire. Do I not chiefly, if not exclusively, seem to myself to be free only when I succeed in using my will in opposition to my own desire—provided, of course, that it is not just a question of a mere whim, but that the will is embodied in acts which themselves form part of what I call reality? From this point of view one might say that the will appears as a resistance to the seductions to which desire exposes me, seductions which, if I yield to them, are quick to turn into compulsions.

We are still, however, I think, falling short of a reality which is much more complex and disconcerting. Let us suppose that I come to realize that in some particular circumstance I yielded to my desires, although I admit that I should not have done so. Would I be right in claiming that I did not act freely? It is a very delicate matter to answer such a question. In order to find some sort of self-justification, or to put it more exactly, in order to shift my responsibility, I should probably be inclined to say that the temptation was too strong for me to resist; that amounts to saying that a power independent of my will tyrannized me, and I was forced to obey. It may prove useful at this point to question what I shall call the legal force of such an assertion. We cannot just make a pure and simple affirmation of its truth or falsity. But I may be forced to conclude that the saving clause in which I took refuge against a particular accusation, does not provide me with the shelter on which I counted. Apart from any metaphor, it was meant to disarm the possible accuser within my own consciousness. Now, it may well be that it does not actually succeed in doing this. Here we meet again the inner plurality on which I laid such stress last year, and without which the very life of consciousness is completely unintelligible. I tried to excuse myself in my own eyes, but there is something in me which refuses to countenance this way of proving my innocence. The symptom of this refusal is a feeling of uneasiness, as though I had to admit that I have no right to locate in something internal (let us say in the circumstances themselves), the responsibility for what was in spite of everything my own act. What sort of a thing is this refusal or protest? If we examine it closely we cannot really focus it, unless we free ourselves from the categories which are nowadays our increasingly strict gaolers, the categories of power or efficiency. If I protest, it is because I have a vague feeling that I cannot win such an acquittal except at the expense of my own being. To put it in a much more concrete way, and in words whose meaning can be more readily grasped, if I allow to my desires, which are in some way detached from me, the power to reduce me to slavery, I put myself more and more at their mercy: almost as a man who has once yielded to the demands of a blackmailer finds that he is caught up in a web from which there is no escape. From the same point of view, we might say that the protest is tied up with the recognition of what I expose myself to if I make this plea of personal irresponsibility. The question then would not be whether the proposition is true or false, which is perhaps a meaningless question, but whether or not it entails consequences which will be fatal, not to what I am at the moment, but to what I intend to be.

The true bearing of these remarks is evidently to enrich but also to obscure the idea I can form of my freedom. I have used the word obscure, but it is only an apparent obscurity. We can use the word in this connection only as opposed to a superficial clarity which is that of the understanding; but in fact this latter clarity is not the one which can throw light on freedom for us; to that extent one has probably good grounds for saying that it is *false* clarity; we can see things by its light, but it cannot be the clarity in which we see ourselves; in so far as we endeavour, I shall not say to think of ourselves, but to make a representation of ourselves which takes things as its model, we make it impossible for ourselves, by definition, to attach the least meaning to the word freedom; we have, accordingly, to take refuge in some determinist conception which implies an active misunderstanding of what we are, of the being which questions its own self when it examines itself as we did at the beginning of this chapter.

A sharply defined conclusion seems to me to emerge from the above analysis. This conclusion is that my freedom is not and cannot be something that I observe (*constater*) as I observe an outward fact; rather it must be something that I decide and that I decide, moreover, without any appeal. It is beyond the power of anyone to reject the decision by which I assert my freedom, and this assertion is ultimately bound up with the consciousness that I have of myself. Jaspers puts it extremely well in his *Introduction to Philosophy* (pp. 61-62);* 'We are conscious of our freedom when we recognize what others expect from us. It is upon us that the fulfilment or shirking of these obligations depends; we cannot, accordingly, deny with any seriousness that we have thus to make a decision about something, and so about ourselves, and that thus we are responsible. Further, anyone who refused to accept this responsibility would *ipso facto* make it impossible for himself to exact anything from other men'. I may add, however, that it will be fatal to try to think of this freedom in terms of causality, though so far we have not reached any precise definition; and as we have just seen, in the whole history of philosophy there has been no more tragic error than that of trying to think of free will in its opposition to determinism; in reality it lies in a completely different plane. I would readily agree that it is meaningless from the point of view of determinism, just as there would be no significance in trying to find a bond of cause and effect between the successive notes of a melody.

* Zurich, 1949.

Reflecting on quite different lines, we may add that freedom can in no way be thought of as a predicate which somehow belongs to man considered in his essence. We commonly express ourselves as though there were a real foundation for the judgment of predication, and we should recognize, accordingly, that it is our business to make a strenuous effort to free ourselves from the verbal forms to which in practice we are obliged to have recourse when we speak of freedom; for we do in fact express ourselves as if it were a predicate which belongs to us (taken as subjects). Ultimately, to say, 'I am free', is to say, 'I am I'. Now the latter assertion either amounts simply to the equation 'I=I', or should be looked at not only as something to be accepted with caution, but as being radically false in some of its bearings; for if we examine ourselves conscientiously, we must admit that there are countless circumstances in which each one of us must say, 'I am not myself; my behaviour is automatic, or I am yielding to social mimicry, and so on'. One might add that this assurance of being myself can be dimmed, as a light can be dimmed, when I undergo a process of alienation of which (we may note parenthetically) marxism has diagnosed only one particular modality. In particular it is clear that there is alienation so soon as there is obsession or a fixed idea. This implies that the state of interior dialogue is reduced and diminished, to give way to a unity of a lower order; and that is what we always see in fanatics. But we must note, from another angle, that the preservation of the interior dialogue is always bound up with the act of keeping oneself open to the other, that is to say with being ready to welcome whatever positive contribution the other can make to me, even if this contribution is liable to modify my own position. We must admit, however, that we can be open to others in this way only on certain conditions. When I am faced by a fanatic, it is impossible for me not to feel on the defensive. This is necessarily so because the fanatic, in as much as he is a fanatic, ceases to be an interlocutor, and becomes only an adversary who handles what he calls his ideas as offensive weapons. The result is that I am forced to find some defensive armour for myself, and as what is properly called discussion is shown to be impossible, I feel bound in the end either to meet violence with violence, or to refuse the battle. I need hardly add that the most serious fault which could be laid to the charge of fanaticism, is that of forcing on its opponents the cruel compulsion of falling themselves into the same fault. The Saint alone, it would seem, can escape this compulsion, but only we may add, provided that his sanctity does not degenerate into weakness, provided that he possesses, on the contrary, the highest degree of that virtue of strength which at present seems to be ill understood by a vast number of Christians.

We see also—and this, I think, is a most significant illustration of the ideas I have been trying to bring to light— that fanaticism is the born enemy of freedom. Not only does it kill freedom in the man in which it dwells, but it has the further tendency to surround itself with a depopulated zone, a no-man's-land.

The sum of these remarks will prepare us, I think, to understand that we must once and for all break with the idea that freedom is essentially liberty of choice—the latter, moreover, being conceived as indetermination. Descartes had already seen this with profound insight. The '*liberté d'indifférence*' is the lowest degree of freedom, and yet it would seem that choice seems most absolute exactly when the reasons for choosing one way or the other are the least strong. One is always inclined to imagine free will as being something that finally tips the scale of a balance which but for this decisive intervention would swing indefinitely. But this is another of those materialist representations which we have constantly had occasion to criticize. It is bound up, moreover, with a conception of motives or motors whose effect is to picture them as forces which display a certain degree of intrinsic intensity, whereas the determining value of these motives or motors depends directly on personality itself.

We must, it appears, assert most emphatically on the one hand that the 'liberté d'indifférence' implies that the stake is insignificant, and on the other hand that we can speak of freedom only when the position is reversed and we can see that the stake has a real importance. The value of the stake, however, has no existence outside my consciousness; though this in no way means, as one might be inclined to say at first blush, that it is *created* by my consciousness. The truth would seem rather to be that I must realize *in concreto* that I should be betraying or denying myself if I failed to set this value on the stake. In this line of thought we must say that the free act is essentially a significant act. But it is impossible not to see that the pointless plays an enormous part in our lives, and that this part is that of the contingent. At this point it would be necessary for us to push our analysis much farther and ask ourselves what is this betrayal or non-betrayal, this denial or non-denial. Shall we say that essentially they turn on an ideal? The notion of ideal, however, is one of those notions which we should be most sparing in calling in to help us, for it is just a convenient word which we use to bring out something which in reality is generally lived or felt rather than conceived or represented. Moreover we must allow for the fact that, as we have already seen, in so far as treason is significant—revealing, that is—it is itself a free act. No doubt one might say that what distinguishes the free act is that it helps to make me .what I am, as a sculptor might carve me, whereas the contingent or insignificant act, the act which might just as well be performed by anybody, has no contribution to make to this sort of creation of myself by myself. To that extent it can scarcely be considered as an act. We must add that the value which constitutes the free act as such will hardly be acknowledged except *a posteriori*: there is no doubt that it is something which reflection will recognize as a value, rather than a sort of immediate evidence accompanying the act at the actual moment of its performance. This entails a wide variety of consequences. I should be sadly deceived if I were to imagine that I am acting freely when I am struggling to realize a certain coherence. When coherence is a goal which I set before myself, there is a risk that it will come between me and myself, and in that case it keeps a certain mechanical character. We should never forget that my position is such that I cannot rightly know who I am and who I shall be: in the same way the artist cannot know exactly what his work will be, before he creates it. It may well take the artist himself by surprise, we might say. The same thing happens on occasion with the free act, by which I mean the act which I come to think of, after the event, as having helped to make me what I am.

Do the above considerations help us to see how freedom and grace fit together? Our first task must be to consider what a gift is. It is in so far as it is a gift that grace can concern us, though for the moment we need not complicate the issue for ourselves by introducing the difficulties of a theological order which are raised by this notion, when it is related to a certain dogmatically given context.

What is a gift? Can it be looked at as a simple transfer? The most cursory reflection will show us that it is more than that. Let us suppose that I make someone a present and he comes to thank me for it. If I cut his thanks short by the laconic remark 'It's only a transfer', my words will affect him like a cold douche. To transfer would be simply to move a certain object, a certain possession, from one account to another. Now, even if this is what happens materially, both I and the recipient see it as the expression of something quite different. To understand this, we have only to consider that any gift is in some way a giving of oneself, and that, however difficult it may be to think of a gift of oneself, such a gift cannot on any showing be compared to a transfer.

We should note, in addition, that the gift has a certain character of unconditionalness. It would be no gift at all, for example, to say to someone, 'I am giving you this house, but only on condition that you make no alteration to it except such as I have specified, or receive in it nobody except such people as I shall give you the names of'. We may go deeper and add that to give with a predetermined end in view, such, for example, as using the beneficiary's gratitude to secure a hold over him, is not giving. To give is not to seduce.

Here we meet a difficulty. If we say that the gift has no precise end beyond itself, must we thereby deny it significance? The answer to that is that we must probably, as Bergson says, reach a higher level than finality. To give is to expand, to expand oneself. But we must be careful not to interpret that phrase in a semi-material way, as though it was the overflow of something that is too full. The soul of a gift is its generosity, and it is manifest that generosity is a virtue—therefore to be carefully distinguished from prodigality. Would not a fairly accurate definition of generosity be *a light whose joy is in giving light, in being light*? There can be no substitute here for the word 'light'. There could be no question of using instead the term consciousness, for example. The property peculiar to light is that of being illuminating, illuminating for others —it goes beyond the boundaries which contemporary philosophy attempts to fix or lay down between the *for self* and the *for the other*. One might even say that this distinction does not exist for light, but that if its joy is in being light it can only wish to be always more so. It knows itself, then, as illuminating; and far from this knowledge being comparable to an enfeebling waste of self, it helps on the contrary to increase its power. Like fire, generosity feeds on itself. There is a possibility, however, of a certain perversion, and we must be careful of this. If generosity enjoys its own self it degenerates into complacent self-satisfaction. This enjoyment of self is not joy, for joy is not a satisfaction but an exaltation. It is only in so far as it is introverted that joy becomes enjoyment.

At first this distinction may seem over-subtle. The best way of understanding it more fully is to think of taking part in an orchestra or a choir. There we should undoubtedly find that joy is fundamentally bound up with a consciousness of being *all together*; which *all together*, moreover, can affect even the consciousness which the organism has of its own functioning, in dancing for example, when that functioning is perfectly synchronized with other energy (synergetic). We may note that enjoyment, on the contrary, always implies a certain retiring within oneself; it would hardly be putting my meaning too strongly to say that, to some degree at least, there is something of onanism in it.

The term 'light' has, moreover, this invaluable advantage that it provides a way of interpreting experiences as different as those of the artist, the hero, or the saint. 'Radiance' is the only word which can express these experiences, and this radiance must emanate from the being itself, taken in its act, its example, or its work.

If we begin by defining human being in a way which excludes the possibility of conceiving this light or this radiance, we may be certain that our definition is false; it will need to be readjusted to meet the true fundamental data.

Let us try to carry further both of these analyses at the same time: that of generosity and that of the comparison between generosity and light; and let us try to envisage how this double analysis might lead us to a metaphysic of light. There is a double relation between generosity and gift. On the one hand, it is generosity which makes the gift possible; it is not the cause of the gift, or, to be more exact, there would be no precise or significant meaning in saying that it is the cause. It would certainly be more exact to say that generosity is its soul. Generosity, however, seems itself to be a gift; this means in the first place, negatively, that it is not something which can be got either from oneself or from another. A thing can be got only by dint of insistence and tenacity, and what one acquires is always the result of an effort. A gift, however, is not a result, it arises spontaneously.

We may thus understand why generosity tends to arouse resentment as well as admiration. The former is always bound up with that turning in on oneself—'Why has he treated me in this way? Why this difference between us? It looks as though he were trying to put me down by forcing me to make this comparison between us. Besides, he isn't doing anything praiseworthy by behaving like this—merit always consists in extracting from poor ground, by dint of hard work, what that ground could not have produced by itself. Admitting, at a pinch, that his ground may be more fertile than mine, yet it is only luck that he has it at his disposal, and there's nothing admirable in luck'.

Just as light can be recognized only through the medium of that which it illuminates—for in itself it is blinding and I cannot look straight at it—so generosity can be discerned only through the gifts it lavishes.

What seems to me most worthy of note in this matter, is that there is a sort of rebound by which to reflect on generosity puts us in a better position for understanding the nature of light; and I am no longer speaking of physical light. One could put it schematically and distinguish three stages: light as a physical agent helps us to think of generosity: but in return as soon as we turn our attention to generosity in its essence, generosity shows us the road to the metaphysical light, which is indeed the light of which St. John speaks as enlightening every man who comes into the world.

So we may see how the road climbs by which we can ascend from the gift considered in its most empiric manifestations to something which can be thought of only as grace.

To sum up and complete these notes, we should consider also the gift from the point of view of the beneficiary. If I am to be certain that something has been given to me and not simply lent, I need a formal assurance; and looked at in this way, the word, whether written or not, may appear as constituting the gift as such. This is true at least for a particular thing which can be designated and whose possessor can be identified. But can that assertion retain any meaning when it is a question either of an inborn disposition—a gift for music or mathematics—or of what is an infinitely more important thing, the fundamental gift: the gift of life, that is, of the fact, with all its concrete applications, of being in the world? for I cannot be in the world without being fitted into it in conditions which are fixed to a certain point or extent in the vast human adventure. Again, is there any significance at all in imagining a word which would in some way guarantee this gift? At first this question may seem disconcerting, and there can be only one possible answer to it: this word can only be a Revelation, without, however, it being necessary for us at the moment to specify in any way the conditions in which this revelation may be introduced. I cannot undertake to give a more precise answer to a question which is still by no means clear to me, and I shall content myself with pointing out that speech itself, human speech, far from being reducible by any transition to spontaneous expression such as we find it among animals, can probably be interpreted only as a reflection of the Word, that is to say, the *Logos*.

Thus it is only in so far as I somehow become gratefully conscious of this revelation that I can come to apprehend life and my own life as a gift. But it is none the less true that this apprehension can exist without my being articulately and distinctly conscious of the Revelation as such. This is the case of those whom one may call naturally religious beings. On the other hand it always remains possible for me to deny myself such a view of life and of my own life: by that I mean that I can interpret either of them as absurd phenomena, freaks, a sort of flaw in the diamond which is Being in itself. In our own day such an interpretation is embodied in the work of Valéry, for example, and in that of Sartre too. For my own part I may say that it presents itself to us as a temptation, like the poisonous berries which a little child is tempted to pick and put in its mouth.

This is an ambiguous way of putting it, however, and may be dangerous. Are we to interpret it as meaning that we have some sort of arbitrary choice between two conceptions of which it cannot rationally be claimed that one is more true than the other? In that case the affirmation of grace would have only a sort of pragmatic value, inasmuch as it would allow us to preserve certain values which we are not prepared to sacrifice. It is impossible, however, not to realize that, inspired by a certain notion of courage and uprightness of mind, any philosopher worthy of the name would be chary of allowing himself to be duped and seduced, and would never be able to resist the temptation to reject grace.

Nevertheless, I am quite sure that the problem cannot be put in these terms. No doubt it is very difficult, if not impossible, to demonstrate that the negative interpretation is false, but in return we can see quite clearly that this same interpretation makes it extremely difficult for us to understand what truth can be, or even, to go deeper, how the term 'truth' can retain any significance.

At this point we should co-ordinate what was said earlier in this chapter about the light which is a joy in giving light, and the conclusions we reached in my first volume about the intelligible medium. From that point of view we should probably be able, not to prove, but to show that the negative interpretation must almost inevitably be self-destructive. It is possible, no doubt, at least verbally to be satisfied with this self-destruction, to enjoy it in a satanic sort of way;

and one cannot, strictly speaking, refute a man who experiences this enjoyment, for the refutation requires at least a minimum of good will in the man who is refuted. It is precisely this good will which is lacking in such a case. But—and here we meet the conclusion to which we are driven—it would still be necessary to enquire whether freedom retains any meaning or value when that good will is no longer present. In that case it shrinks in fact to an anarchical disposition which bears no relation to what a reflective mind can understand by the word and can at the same time regard as a value. Our argument leads us, then, to what seems to me the absolutely essential idea that values—freedom, for example, and truth—cannot be arbitrarily divorced from one another without losing their character; and I may add that they cannot be looked at as values except by a man who has placed himself, if I may so put it, within the axis of intelligible light. By those last words I do not mean a light that could be understood—a meaningless phrase—but a light which is at the root of all and every understanding.

CHAPTER VIII

TESTIMONY

THE views we developed in the preceding chapter have this advantage for us, that they give us considerable help in avoiding any causalist interpretation of grace. It is quite apparent that every critique of grace which implies the notion that grace is a mode of causality distinct from the causality which is proper to the human agent, would miss the point of our enquiry. When I said that generosity is the soul of the gift, I by no means meant that it is its cause, but, what is a very different thing, that it is its active essence. This is the perspective, I think, in which the dispute between the believing philosopher and the atheist should be set. One might perhaps express the question as follows: is there any meaning in maintaining that I am wrong when my *being in the world* appears to me as the expression of a generosity of which it is the embodiment? The atheist's reply to this question is that in reality nobody, no person qualified to bestow that gift on me, exists at all. But an answer, or a question of this sort, is conceivable only when particular verifications are possible: by which I mean that fundamentally they are conceivable only in the sphere where identifiable causes operate; for example, I receive a letter or a parcel, and I should be able to work back to the person who sent it to me; we may note that here we have, in principle, a mutual inter-penetration of causality and finality, but it may also happen that this mutual inter-penetration does not take place—for example if the letter or parcel reaches me only through some mistake. But now that we are dealing with *being in the world*, we find that what we are concerned with is precisely the non-identifiable, as such; and this for the quite obvious reason that no identifications at all can be made except *on the inside* of or within the boundaries of *being in the world*. In the perspective of faith, however, which is at the same time that of freedom, it is this non-identifiable which is experienced or apprehended as the absolute Thou (*Toi*). That may perhaps be too summary a way of expressing it, and it might be better to say that this non-identifiable is seen in a light which is acknowledged as a presence.

But it is impossible not to realize that if a man endorses this scheme, the sort of denial which atheism ultimately reaches seems to miss the point of the question. This is not the end of our troubles, however, for we cannot but ask ourselves whether beyond the verifiable, and, which comes to the same thing, beyond that which can be denied, there still lies reality. There we face the crucial question; we must be most exacting in our approach to it, and there is no doubt that we shall now do well to put it as concretely as possible.

There are times when my own faith seems to me like a stranger: there is a gap between the believing or *praying me* and the *reflecting me*. This cannot be a mere accident. The possibility of this gap between me and myself seems to be implied in what I am, and it is a thing which I must face. In truth, however, the more I look at it, the more I face it, the more do I get beyond the opposition between the two; it is as though a new sort of unity arose between the two aspects of myself which at first seemed antagonistic. Does that mean that we meet again a scheme like that of Hegel's—synthesis following after thesis and antithesis? By no means; on the contrary, I should be inclined to say that in this case even the possibility of synthesis seems to be excluded, nor do I think it any more possible that it may be resolved, in the musical meaning of the word, in some perfect chord: the perfect chord, at any rate, is inconceivable for the wayfarer I am— for the man *on his road to*—which means, fundamentally, for man pure and simple, for a man who was no longer on a road to anywhere would be a man no more.

Nevertheless, even if there can be no question of the perfect chord, there must certainly be room here for a certain harmony, or we might do better to say a certain *modus vivendi*, between the praying and the reflecting me. This means that far from rejecting reflection as he would reject a temptation, the believer should in some way undertake it. To undertake it, however, means in this context, to take to oneself, as one accepts a test, I should rather say an ordeal. In my first volume I devoted considerable space to emphasizing that notion; what is its significance in this context? We may say that to the believer it appears that he must so purify his faith that it can the better resist the attack of reflection, the latter thus becoming the medium, the stimulus which makes this purification possible. In addition, reflection must confirm the legitimacy of a faith which it grasps at first in its most abstract essence. It is on the basis of this double recognition that the *modus vivendi* can be built.

But we must here foresee an objection that is not without weight. One might ask whether this purification does not consist in substituting progressively more abstract terms for the concrete and necessarily hybrid or uncertain terms in which faith was expressed before it had been submitted to this proof. Would not the God of this purified faith in the end be minimized into some abstract entity like Fichte's moral order?

We shall have to show that it would always be a great mistake to understand this purification in such a way, and this by virtue of the realist presuppositions on which we have been led to build the whole of this philosophy. It is true that the more pure cannot but be opposed to the more concrete, but it may be that there is a real concrete, *which is being*, and a pseudo-concrete *which disguises itself* as being.

We have come to a point where it must be apparent that the philosophy of being can in no way be opposed to the philosophy of freedom, as has been thought by those who have modelled their static notion of being on Bergson and have confused being with the thing. This is the root of the serious mistake they made in reducing it to the aspect which it presents to an objectivizing or objectivistic thought. What they failed to do was to understand that objectivizing thought is by definition foreign to the exigence of being, which, as we know, coincides with the exigence of transcendence. It is only from this point of view that we can question ourselves about the true character of the purification we were discussing above. After all, to purify myself, is to make myself more open to this light itself, more liable to being penetrated by it; and yet that even is not putting it strongly enough, it is making myself progressively more capable of giving out this radiance in my own turn.

This would seem more understandable if there were a real certainty that I have been endowed with such a power of dissemination, but with what certainty are we concerned, and on what does it turn? To revert to what I have said about *Being and Having*, I should say that we are concerned here with a certainty which I *am* rather than with a certainty which I have. If I had it, it would be mine to pass on, and we should have to ask ourselves under what conditions such a transmission is possible. In fact I do *not* possess it, not even in the way in which I have a certain knowledge which has been conveyed to me; it is also something which is not in the least degree comparable to an object. But how can I *be* a certainty, if not in as much as I am a living testimony? Truth to say, it would be intolerably presumptuous to claim that I am effectively such a testimony, but I can at least aim at becoming it; and so we may see with much more clarity in what the required purification consists.

This is still not the end of our difficulties, however; we have now to delve further into the essence of testimony. On the empirical plane, the notion of testimony raises no appreciable difficulty. If I say that I have been a witness of a certain occurrence, it means that I have been present at it, that is, that up to a point at least I have been conscious of what happened. Hence there is an active possibility of my asserting sometime, should occasion arise, that I was effectively present when the fact occurred, and of giving some indication about that aspect of it which was clearest to me. One might add that a certain connection has arisen between the fact and my own existence, and this will enable me to say, if it should be necessary to be a witness in court: '*As true as I stand here before you, this is what happened in my sight and hearing*; you can no more challenge my statement than you can deny my presence *hic et nunc*'. Moreover, it is only my word that can frame this connection, but this word is responsible to itself and does not recognize your right to cast doubt on it. It is here that the oath comes in, which is implied by the act of giving testimony,

and which is the word consecrating itself. The word ' consecrate' is of the utmost importance in this context, and that
precisely because of its reference to the sacred. In a world in
which the sense of the sacred has disappeared, the oath becomes
impossible and meaningless; and it is perhaps from this point
of view that we should look at those perversions of judicial
institutions which we can witness today, and that we are able
to realize to what extent the human world as such has been
disrupted.

We must be quite clear that there is no doubt but that it is
on the *historic* that testimony bears. Neither the mathema-
tician nor the physicist as such can be witnesses, and this
arises primarily from the fact that they themselves appear in
some way as the place in which a certain truth is revealed;
and this truth seems, moreover, in some way to suppress or at
least to dismiss as something purely contingent the sort of medium or vehicle of which at a given moment it has had need.
With the witness the contrary is the case: when he comes in
and, because he is a witness, is found to be indispensable, it is he
who supports the testimony and gives it its weight. But it is a
living being who is slipped in at a certain moment in the story;
his existence is extended beyond his own life, but at the same
time he does not cease to be himself. Thus it is, to take the
case which has the most direct interest for us, that the testimony of the martyr continues to be operative after the disappearance of the man who gave it; and this means that the
disappearance is not absolute, so long as something persists:
an oral tradition, a written account, anything which, though
it is not and cannot be outside time, can continue itself or
can perhaps be brought back to light after being eclipsed. We
may well note that even the truth discovered by the scientist

cannot be embodied or passed on without some material support. But ideally—some will say it is a fiction—it still appears as independent of this or of any other support.

One might, it is true, ask whether it is not possible to testify to an idea, that is to say to something which is in itself beyond time. This, however, would seem to be possible only in so far as the idea has been embodied, for example when justice has been violated in the person of the innocent victim of an unjust sentence; and thus we come back to a certain historical datum. To conduct an active campaign for the recognition of the innocence of the victim will be to act as a witness. We must, I think, emphasize that the same cannot be said of the philosopher or the moralist who writes a treatise on justice, unless by so doing he incurs the punishment which tyrants inflict on those who defy them. But here again we are back in the historic.

It is not difficult, I think, to proceed from all these rather elementary considerations to the important idea that in the order which matters to us—that of faith—there can be testimony only of the living God. The God with whom theologians of the traditional type are most frequently concerned, the God whose existence they claim to demonstrate to us, cannot for all that be the occasion of any testimony; and to that extent one might be tempted to say that He cannot concern the believer as such. That God, who is in fact the God whom Pascal calls the Philosophers' God, stands in a dimension which is not and cannot be that of faith. But, if we skip several stages, we are led to ask ourselves whether the living God is not inevitably a God who has become incarnate, and whether it is not to this same incarnation that the testimony is in the first place directed. *Grosso modo* we might put it concretely by saying that if belief in a living God is not to sink into mythology, it means, not exclusively but at least secondarily, that every approach to justice, for example, or to charity, in the person of my neighbour, is at the same time an approach to this God Himself; and this entails an entirely concrete but quite mysterious relation between this living God and this creature who is my neighbour. If this were not admitted, what one maintained to be a living God would thereby be reduced to an idea which is of necessity unalterable and against which I cannot sin. We may note that the introduction of the word 'sin' is inevitable at this point, and moreover that it is clear that since the world of testimony is that of freedom, it is also one in which one can refuse to testify, or else in which one can be a false witness, etc., that is, a world in which there can be sin.

If we carry on this line of thought, we shall understand quite clearly that in the Christian scheme the witness is not only someone who has been a contemporary of Christ in the chronological meaning of the word, or a direct recipient of His teaching. The effect of Incarnation is in fact to spread radiance, and it is just for that reason that today there can still be witnesses of Christ, whose evidence has a value that is not only exemplary but strictly apologetic.

This is not, however, the place in which to develop these corollaries. What is more important is to understand that here we have the interlocking of an historical religion with what could only be religion in general or faith in general, and which is in fact only the priming of a concrete spirituality. But when I speak of interlocking, it must be realized that there can be no question here either of an analytical bond—that is self-evident—or even of any dialectical chain. The philosopher who appreciates the exigence of transcendence in its fulness, that is, who cannot rest satisfied either with what takes place in this world, or even with the world itself considered in its totality—a totality, moreover, which is always fictitious —may nevertheless fall short of conversion to any particular historical religion. In such a conversion there is no movement imposed by necessity, but it must be added that neither is there any free act in the meaning which the word consistently bears, at least if freedom is supposed to be a spontaneous initiative proceeding from myself. Conversion cannot but appear to a man who has not been converted as depending on conditions which are foreign to his will and even strictly impossible to foresee. There is a gap, and it is not man's business to fill it up for himself. Grace will appear before conversion as an incomprehensible power which may perhaps operate, but may also fail to intervene. Let us note that *at a distance*, if I may say so, grace inevitably appears as some sort of a cause; but this is connected with a misconception of grace. This is, moreover, bound up with the fact that an historical religion—and here we must think primarily of Christianity— almost inevitably appears as an object of scandal to one who is not yet a convert. All we can say is that at its furthest extension metaphysical thought perceives the possibility of conversion, but perceives it as being dependent on conditions which it is beyond the power of freedom to bring about by itself. We should certainly add, as a rider to what we said above, that conversion is the act by which man is called to become a witness. This presupposes, however, that something has actually happened in which he will have to discern the action of the living God, or again a recognizable call which he will have had to answer. Here we can put our finger precisely on the interlocking of freedom and grace, and we see how neither can in any way be thought of without the other. But we have reached the point where it must be clear at the same time that we should be making a mistake, were we to try to localize this conversion at a given moment of its duration. The fact or the occurrence to which we give the name conversion, is only the starting point of a movement which must progress without any break. The most serious error of which the converted can become guilty is that of believing that he is placed or installed once and for all in some privileged position from which he can look condescendingly on the tribulations of those who have not yet joined this sort of 'home'. It is just this idea of 'home' which must be rejected with the utmost emphasis, at least if this 'home' is conceived not as a goal, as something to be reached, but as being already dwelt in. The converted, in the only sense of the word we can accept, must realize that there is nothing on this plane which can be won once and for all, that there is a constant possibility of relapse, and that he is in danger of falling much lower even than his original starting-point; and this for the weighty reason that if he relapses he will no longer have the benefit of the sort of allowance that is made for the state of the honest unbeliever.

We may add that any interpretation of this in the language of possession would be radically mistaken. We could also draw certain conclusions from it about the attitude which those who are believers of long standing should adopt towards recent converts. Above all they should be careful not to treat them as recruits, whose enrolment provides them with reinforcements; and it is here that we might well bring out the extreme importance of a certain tact which is connected with the concrete respect or delicacy we have already had occasion to mention. This tact may be well compared, I think, to the precautions which a gardener has to take to ensure the growth of a very delicate plant. But in this case, by an extreme paradox, the gardener has to see himself as a plant exposed to the inclemency of time and habit. By a sort of remarkable inversion, he has to send himself back to the novitiate, so that the conditions under which the novice lives may give him immunity for a time from these inclemencies. Thus there comes about a completely spiritual interaction, which, in as much as it is a life and not just a disposition, has its roots in charity itself. From this point of view the philosopher seems to be better able to distinguish the nature of a *Church*. Ecclesiological reflection should take for its object the bringing to the surface of the implications of this change. It would doubtless allow to emerge, to be developed (as we use the word 'develop' in photography) the existence of a concrete intelligible medium outside of which what we call faith is certainly in danger of being degraded into a rather erratic disposition, or even to an unguided phenomenon which to an external observer would keep a dangerously problematical character.

These are the chief considerations we should take as a starting point from which to try to clarify the conditions or guiding rules for the philosopher who wishes to direct his thought to faith. What is required of him is in the first place to take this question of faith seriously, or, if you like, to acknowledge its reality, even if in all honesty he cannot say that he personally adheres to this faith, and if for some reason ingrained in his nature, the idea of conversion is repellent to him.

We must, however, at this point, anticipate an objection

which threatens the whole basis of our argument: what, then, is the value of this exigence to which the philosopher must bow? By what right do we claim that he must give faith the benefit of a favourable prejudice, instead of keeping a strictly neutral attitude towards it? The very use, however, of the expression 'favourable prejudice' seems to be bound up with a misunderstanding which it is important to clear up; the phrase could only be justified if what we are concerned with were comparable to an hypothesis. Any hypothesis at all should in fact be considered by the philosopher with absolute impartiality. But we must put out of our mind the idea that we are dealing with anything comparable to an hypothesis, and it may well be useful to sum up briefly the reasons for rejection. We spoke of the possibility and even the necessity of a purification in such a sphere. But this implies a participation on the part of the subject which is quite inconceivable in the sphere of knowledge properly so called. Now, an hypothesis can never be anything but a preliminary stage on the road to knowledge. It is valueless except in so far as it is capable of being either confirmed or disproved by experience. We may add that in either case it will cease to exist as an hypothesis. In the case with which we are concerned, anything of this nature cannot be conceived; and to understand this, it is only necessary to recall the nature of the credit which I have opened in favour of the being I love. It would be absurd to say, 'I admit as a plausible hypothesis that he will not deceive me'. If I love him, I lay it down as an axiom that he *cannot* deceive me. It is possible, of course, that I may be mistaken and that I may come to realize my mistake, but this will make no real difference to the fact that I have had faith in this being, and in a sense which transcends every possible supposition. This becomes infinitely more clear when it is a question of the *transcendent Being*, to whom I am compelled to open an absolute, that is to say an unconditional, credit; and we should have no hesitation in saying that the more unconditional my faith is, the more genuine it will be. No doubt—and we cannot emphasize this too strongly—there will be no lack of circumstances which may make me falter; if the being whom I love best in all the world is taken from me in incredibly cruel or brutal circumstances, I shall be unable to refrain from protesting: 'If there were a God . . .'; or, which comes to the same thing, 'If He possessed the attributes with which we commonly endow Him, He would not have allowed this monstrous happening'. But if I yield to this temptation, shall I not thereby reveal that my faith implied an unacknowledged condition? To be sincere, I shall have to realize that what I should have said in the first instance was, 'I shall believe in You, God, in so far as You ensure for me the minimum of moral comfort I need, but not beyond that point'. Then it will be as though I were conscious of having made some contract with God and as though I accused Him of having broken it. To look at it more deeply, it will be as though I said, 'It looks as though this contract had been broken by the other party; what really happened, however, was that the other party did not exist, and I made my contract with an imaginary being; for if he had been real, he could not have brought himself to incur the guilt of such a crime'.

Objectively speaking, there is nothing, indeed, which can prevent me from giving way to this sort of indignation, and here what we said about the relations between freedom and faith is brought out with great clarity. Each one of us, if he examines himself honestly, will have to confess that he is liable to take up such an attitude when overburdened by misfortune. The impulse will be the more irresistible, also, the more his relation to God has not been a living relation, but has been reduced to a collection of abstract theological statements. In such statements there is certainly nothing strong enough to resist the assault of concrete facts. But reflection, whenever it is positive, that is, recuperative, is bound to realize that a being in whom faith really resides, will undoubtedly find, not in himself, indeed, not in his own unaided resources, but by the help of God's own presence, the strength to repel this temptation.

It is true that one could counter by saying, 'So deep a faith can only be a gift of God. How can I be blamed if this gift has not been granted to me?' Again we find that the root of the objection lies in a materialist representation, the picture of some deficiency of supply. In fact, however—and here we face one of the central paradoxes we must particularly stress— if this way of picturing it makes me drive a wedge between my faith and myself which separates me from the thing whose possession is my ultimate aim, I am no longer really speaking about faith nor about grace; I am putting in their place pure fictions, instead of the mysterious and indivisible unity of freedom and grace.

We must, of course, add that everything we have just said has a real foundation in—and is not simply confirmed by—any experience we may have of authentic faith in such witnesses as it is our fortune to meet. We have all known beings in whom faith has withstood trials to which it would have seemed natural for it to succumb; we could have gone further and said that their faith emerged even strengthened from these trials. These are the real witnesses. But it is also true that there is always a possibility of shirking or rejecting testimonies such as these, which make us ashamed of our own lack of faith. Then we shall be induced to put in the notion of some sort of vital lies, in Ibsen's sense, which we say these unfortunate people have had to credit in order to live. To acknowledge these testimonies in the fulness of their significance, is in some way to become witnesses ourselves. We might add that if we do acknowledge them, it is because we are ourselves upheld, however feebly, by the exigence to which these witnesses have, for their part, given a full response.

It goes without saying that our opponent will not agree that he has lost the case: he will retort that the fault in our reasoning lies in arguing from the testimony (fictitiously considered as an effect) to the existence of the being about whom such testimony is given. But the same answer will always hold good: the objection implies a fictitious idea of some exteriority of the witness in relation to that about which he testifies. The Christian idea of an indwelling of Christ in the man who is completely faithful to Him, an idea which corresponds exactly in the religious order to the position which I am trying to define on the philosophical plane, involves a categorical rejection of this purely imaginary way of picturing it. Just as I spoke in my first series of lectures of creative fidelity, so now we are concerned with creative testifying. But we must repeat once more that creation is never a production; it implies an active receptivity, and in this connection any idealist interpretation must be resolutely rejected.

We are progressing, accordingly, towards the idea that a theology which is not based on testimony must be looked at with suspicion; to be more precise, it can hardly have more than a negative import, to which, however, we should be

wrong in attaching too little weight. We may perhaps find
something to illustrate this if we go back to the idea of trial
or ordeal as we have been using it in this chapter.

Again it is the causalist interpretation that we have to rule out.
By that I mean that it would be hopeless to imagine some sort
of celestial schoolmaster who sets real spiritual tests which
his creatures have to take; and it may be profitable to give
more explicit reasons why such a conception would be offensive to religious consciousness. The chief argument seems to
me to be this: the examiner who sets a test treats his subject
not as a being, but as a case—in other words, here we are confronted with purely abstract relations between an expert and the
answers to an expert's enquiries. Fatherhood, however, is
something quite different, and excludes such relations. It is
true that it is always possible for the father to behave as a
schoolmaster or pedantic examiner, but that possibility depends on his having a pretentious self-sufficiency which fatherhood should exclude. Now, it is precisely as *fatherhood in its
purity* that the relation between the living God and the faithful
should be conceived. One might also say that human fatherhood is conceived on the model of divine fatherhood, and not
conversely; but here we are concerned with fatherhood taken
in its full richness. If we want to clarify these ideas, we have
only to compare the father in the parable of the prodigal
son with the Roman *paterfamilias*. In the parable fatherhood
appears in what I may call its supra-juridical fulness, and that is
precisely why we can see it as being divine instead of consist-
ing in simple relations of power and right, or in a mere bodily
belonging as considered from the sociological point of view.
We may add that even if we were to find in pre-christian or
extra-christian history some example of paternal love as it

shines through the parable, we should have to see in it only glimmerings through space and time of the pure light which lies at the heart of the gospel.

But if we refuse to think of trial as a contrivance of which God makes use, what becomes of its metaphysical status? We must, I think, say that we can think of circumstance—accident, for example—only as a link in some chain of events. But this is relative to a particular way of conceiving the world, the way of thinking which is chosen or adopted by a consciousness careful to depersonalize itself as much as possible. From the ultimate metaphysical point of view the mistake lies, no doubt, in raising this type of thought to an absolute position. We must keep in mind the possibility of other interpretations. I have often found it useful to take an illustration from music, and I shall do so again; I can to some extent analyse an orchestral score without the meaning of the music being completely grasped by me—the word *meaning* is of course inaccurate, let us rather say the gist of it; by which I mean that the music may *say nothing to me*. It is still foreign to me; I stop short at describing it, though my description may be as minute as you please. But for depersonalized thought accident enters into the matter, in conditions which are capable of being reconstructed objectively, e.g., the motor-cyclist was riding too fast, he did not pay attention to the lights, and so on. Similarly, a discord can be interpreted in a merely contrapuntal way by a technician who does not recognize its musical value; whereas a musician does not see it as in any way contingent, but rather as the expression of an inner necessity to which, however, no strictly logical character can be attached. At the same time, this comparison itself falls far short of adequacy. We are so situated in the world that it is impossible for us to raise ourselves on this earth to a mode of understanding events which allows their intimate meaning to be intuitively apparent to us. The most one could say—and that only tentatively—is that as we approach the apparent term of our existence we are progressively more capable of seeing ourselves in a light which allows the hidden meaning of events to filter through. This light, however, appears to us only in so far as we withdraw from these events in order to penetrate more and more deeply into a reality which is certainly already that of the after life; but it seems true that this grace is given to us only if we come to such self-detachment as will suffice to safeguard us from an impatient anxiety about what is left of our lives—as a man feverishly counts the little money that stands between him and complete penury. Again, of course, we see the opposition between being and having. But do these remarks help us towards an understanding of trial as such? At any rate they show that trial must be looked upon in the light of different perspectives, according to whether we are standing at the exact moment in which it is experienced, or on the contrary, are looking at it retrospectively. When I am faced by a trial, that is to say by something of which I feel at first that I cannot live through it, though it is true that I cannot retrace my steps, I can at least try to avoid it, even if only by suicide. I can also try to clear the obstacle, to climb over it, and this task implies a sort of spiritual equivalent to muscular adaptation. But the more I stake on this action or series of actions, the less I shall feel the need of ratiocinating on the nature of its supposed cause. This ratiocination has nothing in common with a religious attitude; it is even its contrary. This in no way means that I am not called upon to pray, but this prayer turns on the assistance without which it seems to me that I shall not overcome the obstacle. Of course, if I try to form a picture for myself of this assistance, I cannot but think of some contributory force conceived more or less accurately on the model of that which I experience in daily life. But it will be the proper part of reflection to free me from that sort of temptation. It may well be that this liberating reflection is itself moved by grace; left to my own resources, I could not perhaps hope to benefit by its full operative power. I do not offer this remark as a dogmatic statement, but it may help to clarify the function of philosophical thought itself. And we may note in addition that retrospection is always in some degree philosophizing, and that it, too, can (though by different means) overcome what I may call the causal obsession.

Let us remember that for the philosopher everything is in some way a trial; how can he fail to be almost overwhelmed by the disconcerting multiplicity of the empiric data which he has to take into account, by the fear of falling into arbitrary simplifications? Nevertheless, it is his duty to overcome such fears: there is such a thing as philosophical courage.

As we proceed, we shall see that the philosopher seems to be submerged by the variety of aspects disclosed by this protean evil which speculative thought has always been at such pains to reduce to unity; for if there is an evil which comes from privation, from a lack of being, we must also ask, as Kant and Schelling asked, whether there is not a positive evil which is bound up with some radical perversion of will. It is doubtful whether even the most speculative reflection can progress in such a sphere, if it is not what I may call magnetically charged or driven from within by something which is beyond itself and which it is beyond its power to give a complete account of.

Here we see again the indissoluble knot which unites freedom and grace, and which lies at the heart of all these ponderings of ours. On the other hand, this is the first time that we are faced by what has so inaptly been called the problem of evil. The fact that the religious question, as it presents itself to modern consciousness, is undoubtedly inseparable from some sort of taking into consciousness of the problem of evil—we need not necessarily say of sin—makes it the more important for us to reach a sharply defined position with regard to this point. I shall take this opportunity to lay it down as a principle, though my statement is subject to later elucidation, that evil and death can in a certain sense be regarded as synonymous. It is true that one can imagine an unhistorical world in which after the creature had actualized all its possibilities, it would sleep an endless sleep of peace, a world in which natural euthanasia would be the rule and death would no longer be an object of terror. We need not try to ask whether such a world is possible in the abstract. What is practically certain is that that world would lack any spiritual depth; it would be a fairy story world—at that a dreary one—which is certainly not our world. We must recognize that our own world harbours seemingly inexhaustible possibilities of waste and destruction; if we met a man who seemed to us to have reached the fulfilment of his being, and even if grace dwelt within him, such a being would not only not receive therefrom any immunity against the principles of death in the working of our universe; he might well, on the contrary, seem to be even more threatened, even more vulnerable, than average beings, as though his very perfection brought on him the active hostility of some adverse power. I have said, 'as though', because that is actually a mythological interpretation which could not be accepted without falling into Manicheanism. It does not, however, lack a relative consistency which it would perhaps be a mistake to lose sight of entirely; we shall have to meet this again in my last chapter, when we discuss the historic and trans-historic.

CHAPTER IX

DEATH AND HOPE

THE task of constructing anything resembling an ontology
of death is not one that need occupy us now; and it might,
moreover, prove an impracticable one. We must recognize,
also, that the two words go ill together, and what we have
said about *being* is enough to show us why. One might say that
if death has some kinship with life, this is an aspect which remains hidden from us. But whatever may be the ultimate
reality which may lurk behind this terrifying mask, it is none
the less true that for the human being which I am, this assumed
mask is *not* only a mask; and there is no doubt but that the
appalling error of which a certain sort of spiritualism is guilty,
lies in denying to death this gravity, this at all events *apparent*
final value, which gives to human life a quality of tragedy
without which it is nothing more than a puppet-show.

There is a mistake which balances this one; it is even more
serious and much weightier with consequences; it is that
which lies in a dogmatic affirmation of the final character of
death. Later we shall have to deal with this at length; for the
error—which in its origin is more than error, a sin—seems to
be the root from which spring the most terrible of the evils
from which humanity suffers today.

It is between these two errors that we have to pick our way;
and we shall find our path is as thickly strewn with obstacles as
those we have had to follow hitherto. These two converse

errors, moreover, are not simply complementary; there is a direct connection between them. On the one hand, the man who has been offered the too facile, the cheap consolations of a pseudo-religious spiritualism, is liable to be driven by them, if he is disappointed, into helpless despair. But there is a reciprocal reaction; this despair is so intolerable that, failing a religion worthy of the name, there is a danger that it may drive the human being to a search for any sort of refuge at all, and that in practices that are often extremely crude. If we are to avoid the guilt of a blindness which is simply cowardice, what we must keep before our minds with all our strength, is that we are surrounded by possible sources of despair. I would be tempted to say that these possibilities spring up beneath our feet like the riotous and malignant growth of a bewitched jungle. This has always been true, but such a truth is much more noticeable in our day than in any earlier historical period. It may be well for us to ask ourselves why this is so.

There is some ambiguity, too, in asking *why*. Truth to say, I do not think it is at all possible for us to look at this fact from a strictly theological point of view, and ask ourselves what is the higher purpose this swarm of threats and evils may serve. It is true, no doubt, that some will be able to look on it as the realization of some prophecy in a particular sacred book, such as the Apocalypse, for example. But we must look at it in a perspective in which we have to disregard such writings and revelations. The most we can do, and even in this we must be extremely cautious, is to try to define in the abstract the conditions under which, for some people, such prophecies can acquire a truly compelling value. What is immediately obvious is that whenevever circumstances prevailing here and now lead to men being not only regarded as masses but actually treated as such—treated, that is, as aggregates, whose elements are transferable according to the demands of temporal vicissitudes—it becomes more and more difficult to keep in mind the inalienable characteristics of uniqueness and dignity which have hitherto been considered as attributes of the human soul created in the image of God. To say that these characteristics are becoming more and more lost to view is not enough; they are being, if one may so put it, actively denied, they are being trodden upon. Man may end by imagining that he can prove by his very behaviour that he is not such a being as the theologians have defined.

If we look at the question carefully we shall see, also, that we have here a real vicious circle. *The less men are thought of as beings in the sense which we have already tried to define, the stronger will be the temptation to use them as machines which are capable of a given output*; this output being the only justification for their existence, they will end by having no other reality. There lies a road which runs straight to the forced labour camp and the cremation oven. Here we must stress a paradox to which we cannot, I think, direct our attention too closely; theoretically one might have imagined—and this indeed was what many people did in the nineteenth century—that as soon as the majority of men in a given society ceased to believe in an afterlife, life in this world would be more and more lovingly taken care of and would become the object of an increased regard. *What has happened is something quite different, the very opposite in fact: this cannot, I think, be over-emphasized.* Life in this world has become more and more widely looked upon as a sort of worthless phenomenon, devoid of any intrinsic justification, and as thereby subject to countless interferences which in a different metaphysical context would have been considered sacrilegious.

To reflect on this will accordingly lead to the disclosure of an extraordinarily close connection between something which is after all a metaphysical judgment properly so called (*a Weltanschauung*, if you like, though that is always a rather vague term), and a dehumanizing way of behaving which must inevitably, in a world which is more and more enslaved to the demands of technocracy, become universal—or at least which runs the risk of becoming universal. Hence it is that those minds which have progressively lost any capacity for reflection and who have no suspicion of what faith can be, have a way of looking at things which is so consistent that it does indeed become reality for them. By that I mean that it in some way consolidates itself more and more and ends by presenting a formidable character of irreducibility. Under whatever form slavery may manifest itself—the forms it takes are not all equally monstrous, but it is only too clear that the totalitarian countries have no monopoly of them—the fact that it is becoming so widespread is certainly the most glaring fact in a world which is thus consigned to death. Consigned to death—by that I mean without the power to resist the mesmeric power which death exerts over the man who has come to look on it as the final word.

This objection, it is true, may be raised, that those who are the most emphatic in their denial of personal immortality, give themselves out to be the heralds of a glorious future which is not that of the individual, but of the species or of a particular deified society—Nazi Germany or Soviet Russia. Nobody would deny that the hope of this future has acted as an extremely powerful lever in moving an infinite number of people who have been oppressed and have fought with the

utmost bravery against these inhuman conditions, and that by
its aid they have literally been raised above their wretched fate
in this world. At the same time we should, as I have said
before, contrive to understand through a sort of sympathy
which illuminates it, what one might call the internal aspect
of a sacrifice. The fact is, that if we confine ourselves to its
external appearance, we have no answer to give to the man
who says that it is ludicrous to sacrifice one's life in order to
promote the future development of a world one will never
see. But everything that we said earlier about faith has prepared us to understand that faith is infinitely more than a state
of consciousness, and that it is impossible to reduce it in any
instance to a very vague feeling, or to the even vaguer picture
of it which the man may have who has been granted a share of
it. In so far as he is a believer, he is perpetually beyond himself,
and by *himself* must be understood what I shall call his imagina-
tive equipment, which as a rule is after all very limited. To
take a very simple example: the man who sacrifices himself
for his child is in reality possessed by a faith whose content
he cannot in the first place make clear: this faith turns on a
certain supra-personal unity between his child and himself.
To put it more simply, I would say that he feels sure, without
knowing it—and perhaps *essentially* without knowing it—
that there will not be an end of him, but rather that he will
survive in his child. Moreover, what I have said must be taken
in a sense which is at once deeply mysterious and extremely
precise. For what it must mean is a participation (according to
modes of existence which we need not conceive in detail) in
the reality for which he has sacrificed himself. There can be
no justification for sacrifice, it cannot even be thought of,
except *from the point of view of an ontology which is rooted in*

intersubjectivity; looked at in any other way it is a snare and a delusion. We must, in short, state as categorically as possible, even though we shock some semi-agnostics whose reflection is faulty or who often have not reached the depths of human experience, that it is on the ground of immortality that the decisive metaphysical choice must be made.

I should even go so far as to put it like this: if it is true that human beings—we may leave on one side for the moment the much more obscure question of other living beings—must be looked on as interconnected by relations of simple succession, as appearing only to disappear like an interminable game of skittles, then Macbeth's famous words would have to be taken as the literal truth, and the only answer we should have to nihilism would be phrases whose emptiness is apparent as soon as man is faced not, let us say, by his own death (for there is no doubt that in the great majority of cases that is easier to accept than one imagines), but by the death of the being he loves. I may digress for a moment to say that this was the point on which, at the 1937 Congress, I found myself uncompromisingly at variance with the man who was then the foremost representative of critical idealism in France—Leon Brunschvicg; and I have had reason in more than one country to know that this deeply significant discussion made a profound impression on the memories of its hearers. Brunschvicg accused me, though with the utmost courtesy, of laying much more stress on the fact of my own death than he was inclined to put on that of his. My answer was that the right setting of the question was quite different, it lay exclusively in the plane of love.

In a world in which the arid influence of technique seems to prepare the radical disappearance of intersubjective relations, death would no longer be a mystery, it would become a raw fact like the dislocation of some piece of mechanism. In fact, however, this world deserted by love is not our world, it is not yet our world; and it depends on us whether it will ever be so, even though we may see the daily increase in strength of conscious and malignant forces—malignant because conscious—which seem to have set as their goal the creation of this soulless world. I may add, though it is in any case self-evident, that to the eye of any faith worthy of the name, this soulless world can appear only as the wholly sacrilegious experiment of a will for de-creation. It may be, too, that it is as a function of this idea of de-creation (which it would be well to analyse in detail) that one may best understand what I laid down as a sort of postulate at the end of my last chapter, the identity, that is, of evil and death.

Even though these perspectives may conform to those we have taken up since the beginning of our enquiries, yet we cannot hide from ourselves their disconcerting nature. We must, however, deal with an objection which at first may seem overwhelming: it may well be asked how can we speak of choice in this connection, when what we are concerned with is a question of fact. We seem to be saying that the modern world has chosen death, but should one not rather say that under the impulse of positive science on the one hand, and perhaps also on the other, of a philosophy which on the whole one may describe as critical, the keenest minds have been forced to discard as imaginary the dreams of the beyond, of the so-called hereafter, in which our ancestors found consolation? There will be some who will take up a different point of view and add that they would consider it excessively unwise to tie the fate of religion to a belief in a fact as problematical and improbable as survival—not only imprudent but even spiritually illegitimate, since preoccupation with survival is still ego-centric, whereas a religion worthy of the name finds its centre in God and in God alone.

We must make a careful examination of these two points, and try to disclose the confusions which lie at the root of such objections.

In the first place, may we legitimately say that immortality is really either a fact or just a delusion? Can we maintain in this connection the opposition between real and imaginary which takes place whenever our judgement refers to empirical data? Can belief in immortality be likened to a simple mirage? To make such a claim would mean, indeed, that we had completely failed to understand the views we put forward about faith and about what it must inevitably be when it is genuine.

Let us try to keep this as concrete as possible. First let me quote again what one of my characters says, 'to love a being is to say, "Thou, thou shalt not die" '. But what can be the exact meaning or relevance of such a statement? It certainly cannot be taken simply as a wish, a choice; the emphasis of it is that of a prophetic assurance. But on what guarantee could one base such an assurance? From the point of view of the empiricist or positivist it could only be considered absurd, for is it not in effect in formal contradiction with the data of experience? The being I love is exposed to all the vicissitudes to which things are liable, and there is no doubt that it is in so far as he participates in the nature of things that he himself is subject to destruction. But here we must proceed with great caution: the whole question— and it is certainly an extremely obscure one—turns upon knowing whether this destruction can overtake that by which this being is truly a being. Now, it is this mysterious quality which is aimed at in my love. I am ready to admit, too, that here the term 'quality' is inadequate; quality is a predicate, and we have repeatedly insisted that ontology transcends all logical predication; it is here more than anywhere else that speech reaches a deadlock. We must fully realize that this being whom I love is not only a *Thou*; in the first place he is an object which comes within my view, and towards whom I can effect all the operations whose possibility is included in my condition of physical agent. He is a *that*, and it is precisely to that extent that he is a thing; in so far, on the other hand, as he is a *Thou*, he is freed from the nature of things, and nothing that I can say about things can concern him, can concern the *Thou*. There is no doubt that this gives rise to serious difficulties. Are we not restoring, in precarious and danger-ously ambiguous conditions, the traditional distinction between *noumenon* and *phenomenon*? Does not all this simply amount to saying that only the *phenomenon* is subject to destruction, while the *noumenon* is indestructible? Such an interpretation, how-ever, implies a very profound misunderstanding of what we have just said. The fact is, that the *noumenon* is still a *that*, and we shall always be justified even in asking ourselves whether we have there anything but a pure fiction elaborated by ab-stract thought from the basis of the empirical datum. It is not, I think, from the noumenal point of view that the indestructi-bility of the loved being can be affirmed: the indestructibility is much more that of a bond than that of an object. The pro-phetic assurance of which I spoke above might be expressed fairly enough as follows: whatever changes may intervene in what I see before me, you and I will persist as one: the event that has occurred, and which belongs to the order of accident, cannot nullify the promise of eternity which is enclosed in our love, in our mutual pledge.

We cannot fail to see, however, that the notion that something like this is implied, may itself give rise to very serious objections. Even if it is agreed that the act by which beings who love one another are united by a common bond implies within itself the inherent need for eternity (*Ewigkeitsforderung*), what enables us to say that this need is met in some substratum of reality which eludes our sight?

The first thing which one might perhaps underline is that this idea of a substratum is a sort of remnant of a certain realism which itself has never ceased to depend to some extent upon a vague notion, the notion of a materialism in which what is spiritual is incised in durable grooves like those which a needle engraves in a wax disc. But what we have to deal with here is in reality the metaphysical status of hope, of hope taken in its specific character, as opposed to desire.

It may be better however, to examine the second objection first, the objection which is formulated in the name of a theocentric conception of religion.

What we have to find out is whether one can radically separate faith in a God conceived in His sanctity from any affirmation which bears on the destiny of the intersubjective unity which is formed by beings who love one another and who live in and by one another. What is really important, in fact, is the destiny of that living link, and not that of an entity which is isolated and closed in on itself. That is what we more or less explicitly mean when we assert our faith in personal immortality. What we must do, then, is to discover whether I can assert that this holy God is capable either of ignoring our love, of treating it as something accidental or devoid of significance, or even of decreeing its annihilation.

It is abundantly clear that in any sort of pantheist perspective the first hypothesis would seem completely plausible. But the reason for this is that in this same line of thought God after all is simply naturalized. The very notion of pantheism, from the point of view which I have taken up, cannot but give rise to the most profound mistrust, for, as we have already seen and cannot emphasize too strongly, the category itself of totality is strictly inapplicable to what is spiritual. Now, all our work has lain precisely in sketching out some features of a philosophy of the spirit. The living God, who is the God of faith when faith does not degenerate into opinion or superstition, can only be spirit; though that does not mean that this formula should be interpreted in a strictly idealist sense. All things considered, it is towards a realism of mind that all our line of thought is directed; and we should add that these words can attain their full significance only in the light of intersubjectivity, that is, of love. But is it conceivable that a God who offers Himself to our love, should range Himself *against* this same love, in order to deny it, to bring it to nothingness? It is true that we must make full allowance for the absolute incommensurability between that which is by essence infinite and that which belongs to the domain of the created; from this point of view one might sometimes be inclined to pass the harshest, the most depreciatory, judgment on what we may call private loves. But does not this also still imply a confusion, which arises from the fact that when we pronounce this judgment we have not definitely put aside the consideration of the *that*, which is to say of the thing? Now, we must assert as forcibly as possible that human love itself is nothing, it lies to itself, if it is not charged with infinite possibilities. That phrase, however, entails an extremely precise significance: its very exact meaning is that if human love is centred on itself, if it sinks into a mutually shared narcissism, it turns into idolatry and pronounces its own death sentence. Here again we find the inexhaustible fertility of Bergson's distinction between *closed* and *open*. Here, too, we may see the dangerous ambiguity in the notion of the 'pair of lovers', the source of so much bad writing. There is always a danger that that notion may give rise to the sort of self-complacency which makes it into a closed system. By that it shows that it is not from God; the survival of the ego which it demands might very well be no more than an object of desire, and could not accordingly be credited with the status of hope to which we alluded above.

I may add, too, that from the point of view of a doctrine of intersubjectivity, there can be no apparent reason at all for setting an exclusive value on the relation which is built up by man and woman united in the bond of marriage. A friendship, or *a fortiori*, a filial relationship, may also be the road which leads beyond the earthly horizon. I may point out, too, incidentally, that there may perhaps be no significance in attributing a *literally* supraterrestrial character to the invisible in which the intersubjective destiny is fated to develop and fulfil itself. There is no doubt that it is infinitely more reasonable to admit that if the word *beyond* has any meaning—and this we cannot possibly deny—the word cannot be strictly applied to some other place at which one could arrive on leaving this earth. It would be better to follow the indications which we find for example, in Mr. Stewart White's works, and think that what we loosely call 'beyond' consists of unknown dimensions or perspectives within a universe of which we apprehend only the one aspect which is in tune with our own organo-psychic structure.

An 'open' thought is by its essence directed towards this unknown. But we must realize the danger of a baleful confusion arising between what one might call the will for exploration, of which a certain curiosity may be the outcome, and hope properly so called. I should readily grant that it is only by denouncing this possible confusion that one may succeed in tracing the boundary line between the psychic domain and the order of religion. Curiosity, indeed, cannot be divorced from desire, and I have often had occasion to draw attention to the necessity of distinguishing between desire and hope. That point is the more worthy of note, in that Spinoza, in his *Ethics*, when opposing fear to hope and handling them as antithetical data, seems to have made the very mistake that I think we should unmask in this connection. The fact is that desire and hope are to be found in completely distinct spheres of spiritual life. The opposite of hope is not fear, it is a state of dejection; and it can, moreover, appear under a wide variety of psychological species. But in a quite general way one may say that it is the state of a being who expects nothing either from himself, or from others, or from life. There is nothing here which resembles fear; there is rather an immobilization of life; we might say that life is congealed or frozen. It may also happen that the human being takes pleasure in this state, and that is precisely what we can see in some nihilists of our own day. Fear, on the contrary, like desire itself, is bound up with expectation.

Wherein, then, lies the difference between desire and hope? We shall be in a better position to determine this if we remember that in Christian ethics hope is regarded as a

virtue in the same way as faith and charity. How is this possible?
One might point out in the first place that hope is akin to courage. But what sort of courage is meant? There, indeed, we
have a notion which is much more ambiguous than is commonly imagined. As one of my own characters says, one can be
brave in the face of suffering, or even in the face of death, and
yet not be brave in the face of judgment, by which I mean in
face of the notion which others might form of us. One might say
that in every instance courage consists primarily in facing
something. But in the case with which we are concerned, to
face is in some way to deny, or more exactly to reduce to
nothingness (*néantiser*), to use a neologism of Sartre's which
has no precise equivalent: it means, in brief, to treat something actively as neither existing nor being of any account.
The soldier who defies death behaves as though death were of
no account. Let us be aware, however, of a very subtle
shade of meaning which ought not to be overlooked. Bravery
by no means consists in deluding oneself about a given situation.
It reaches its zenith, on the contrary, when the situation is
most clearly appreciated. We might be inclined, then, to say
at first that it is a question of a negation turning on value and
not on existence. At the same time we have already realized
that the opposition between existence and value cannot be
regarded as absolute. Fundamentally it is precisely this
opposition which hope transcends, which, in a certain sense,
it denies. The man who has hopes of the coming a world in
which justice will be paramount does not confine himself to
saying that such a world is infinitely to be preferred to an
unjust world—he proclaims that this world *shall come* into
existence; in this lies the prophetic nature of hope. But by
this, too, we may see more clearly in what courage, which is

the driving force behind hope, truly consists.

During the last war I devoted much thought to the characteristics of hope and to the tragic state of prisoners of war. I concluded by asking myself whether in the last analysis hope might not always be looked on as an active reaction against a state of captivity. It may be that we are capable of hoping only in so far as we start by realizing that we are captives. Our slavery, moreover, may take very different forms, such as sickness or exile. (This will help us to understand why it is that in some countries where social technique is over-developed, in which a sort of ease is assured to everyone, hope fades and withers, and with it the whole of religious life. Life stands still and there is nothing that does not labour under an invincible boredom. This seems to be so in Sweden, to a large extent.) From this it would appear that at the back of hope lies some sort of tragedy. To hope is to carry within me the private assurance that however black things may seem, my present intolerable situation cannot be final; there must be some way out. At this point, there are some complementary notes which cannot be omitted.

The first and perhaps the main point is that this assurance cannot just be overlaid on something inert. The being who hopes is putting forth a sort of interior activity, even though it may not be easy to define the nature of that activity. Once again intersubjectivity will be found to supply the key to the riddle. It is well to bear in mind the ordeals of those whose country was for a time enslaved and who yet persisted in their hope of liberation. Hope was not simply a hope for one's own self; it meant spreading one's hope, keeping its flame a radiance of hope burning around one. We may go further and say that it is probably only by so doing that a man can keep it alive in the depths of his own being. But, as we have already seen, each man's personal reality is itself intersubjective. Every man finds within him another self which is only too inclined to give up the struggle and despair; thus it is that in his own interior citadel he has to exert the same effort as in the so-called exterior zone in which he is in communication with his neighbour. A sick man who hopes he will recover, does not simply wish to be cured. He does not stop short at saying, 'I wish I could be cured'; he tells himself, 'You shall be cured', and it is precisely when this happens that such a hope can sometimes become a real factor in the cure. It may be objected, of course, that there we have auto-suggestion pure and simple; and the attack could be pushed further by saying that when this auto-suggestion brings about external effects, there is no change in its nature. But at this point we should try to disclose the postulates on which a man bases himself when he speaks of auto-suggestion in this depreciatory tone. What he is doing in fact is to contrast it as a sort of simply illusory operation—what I would be prepared to call an auto-mystification—with what is a real process which develops autonomously; we should note, too, that even when we are discussing auto-suggestion, a certain empiric efficacy is attributed to this despised operation, and we are justified in asking how we are to account for this efficacy itself, this grip on real facts.

But there is more to be said. Even as far as the idea of suggestion can be regarded as self-consistent, it is extremely doubtful whether it corresponds to the reality with which we are concerned. Auto-suggestion consists, to put it briefly, in closing oneself in on a certain representation: it is difficult to think of it except as a psychic contraction. But, on the contrary, we cannot but think of hope as an expansion: it implies an *open time* as opposed to a *closed time* in the contracted soul. But this can be seen clearly, I think, only in connection with the actual idea that one forms of hope; and in this new context we rediscover what we said earlier about conversion; for the latter seems without doubt to consist in the somehow mysterious passage from the closed time to the open time. It could be demonstrated, moreover, that this closed time is not necessarily that of despair which sees nothing before itself and which expects nothing from anybody: it can as well be that of a man who is shut in in the circle of his daily tasks, who is chained by the fetters of routine. He may, indeed, despair, but he is not aware of it; he will not become conscious of it until he has freed himself from the jaws of this vice.

No doubt there will be some who will feel unable to master their impatience and will ask us what is this hope and to what is it directed. Is it to a solution of our difficulties in this world? Or is it on the contrary to a development in the unseen which will perhaps take its start only after death? In the first case, there is always the danger that hope will meet with the direst disappointment; in the second, it passes into the sphere of the unverifiable; we shall always be entitled to see in it a mere mystification, even a sheer swindle.

The first answer, I think, must be this; to hope is not essentially *to hope that* . . . whereas to desire is always to *desire something*. I once wrote that hope is the stuff of which our soul is woven. But would it not be possible for hope to be another name for the exigence of transcendence, or for it to be that exigence itself, in as much as it is the driving force behind man the wayfarer? Could it be claimed that to conceive of hope in this way is to confuse it with life itself? A word of warning, however: the idea of life itself is ambiguous. It may apply to a simple process which can give rise to description and analysis. Every human being can dwindle into a condition which is in some way akin to the vegetable: biologically speaking, they are alive, but spiritually they are dead. On the other hand we have all met people who remained alive in the spiritual sense until the verge of death, and when their physical strength seemed utterly exhausted.

Here, however, we are confronted by a paradox. By this I mean that it seems, at least as far as man is concerned, that even if life is weakened and in a way degraded, it must still retain a certain character of sacredness; otherwise there would be no reason for doubting the legitimacy of the treatment which supporters of euthanasia claim they may apply to incurables. The majority of civilized beings are impelled to protest against such practices, and their protests cannot but be regarded as a *danger signal* to arrest us on the slope down which contemporary man is in danger of sliding. It is in fact a warning to remind us of the sacred element which is inseparable from any and every human existence. It may, of course, be held that this warning is only a survival, and that it is the part of reason to expose the antiquated character of such a mental attitude. Here again we are faced by an inescapable dilemma. But the fact is that if this consciousness is enfeebled, the road is open to terrifying mismanagement. We must accordingly realize, I think, that here we are faced with a certain absolute, and that this absolute must be assisted, however strong the temptation may be to reject it.

The conclusion of all we have just said seems to be twofold —we must acknowledge the profound ambiguity of what we call life and at the same time emphasize, in a darkness in which there is otherwise hardly a glimmer of light, the incomprehensible unity of aspects which at first we thought should be dissociated. We shall, I think, find the least inadequate interpretation of this unity, if we interpret it as an expression of a divine gift. At the same time it may be that we should allow a predominantly negative import to this interpretation; it is primarily the rejection of an objectivizing representation, even if it seems impossible to remove from the words we are obliged to use any traces of such a representation.

A myth, again, such as that of the phoenix, might help us at this point: we could say that all life holds within itself a promise of resurrection. However strong may be my motives in suppressing life, the act of suppression may imply a sacrilegious attempt at interrupting a certain cycle, or even the actual will to bring it to a final term. To kill is in the first place to wish to suppress; it implies the intent to destroy what is perhaps in itself indestructible. Such an intent is at once sacrilegious and profoundly absurd. This circuitous approach may perhaps lead us to see more clearly wherein hope is akin to life, when life is looked at, not in its manifestations, but in its essence, which is perhaps a certain perennialness. A world such as our own, in which murder on an almost incredible scale is growing common, a world which seems soaked through and through with crime, such a world cannot but be increasingly impervious to hope. Some may see in this but a hackneyed commonplace, to others it will be a paradox that can hardly be maintained; it is only the latter point of view that we need deal with at the moment.

In totalitarian countries, which nowadays try to impose their rule upon the whole world, men seem to claim that there is an obligation to sacrifice whole generations in order to ensure the advent of a just society. Surely, then, some fanatics will contend, it is here that hope reaches its climax? The answer is, no: that is a ghastly lie; it is despair wearing the mask of hope, and it is that mask that we have to tear away. Once more we must pay heed to the existence of hidden connections which, indeed, we can always break up; but let us remind ourselves that values really hang together, and it is a hopeless undertaking to try to promote justice at the expense of truth—that is to say, of justice itself. A human future which is founded on the deliberate extermination of millions of individuals can only be corrupt in its own principle, and it is that future which we must wholeheartedly reject. What exactly are we to understand by this refusal? It is not just a matter of reciting professions of faith or of signing manifestos —these are mere gestures. We must disclaim any complicity, even tacit; and that means that our action has to exert itself in an entirely different dimension.

In the last chapter of this series, we shall have to make an effort to define more precisely what this dimension can and should be, and to show that what matters today is that man should rediscover the sense of the eternal, and withstand those who would make his life subservient to an alleged sense of history.

CHAPTER X

CONCLUSION

I SHOULD wish this last chapter to be like the finale of a symphony, in which I shall try to bring together the principal themes which have followed one another during the course of these lectures. Needless to say, I shall not be satisfied simply by a sort of summing up. What I wish to do, if I may so express it, is so to state these themes that each may become aware of the importance they hold for his own life.

Let me digress at this point. There have been periods in history when a philosopher's audience could listen to him in a certain atmosphere of serenity. They could look upon their future on this earth as being comparatively safe, not, of course, from the accidents to which every individual life is exposed, but at least from the great historical cataclysms which, by an odd optical illusion, already seemed to belong to the past. Such was the case, for example, during a great part of the nineteenth century. But our situation today is precisely the opposite. Without there being any question of prophesying or of simply giving way to a fatalism which, for my part, I consider unlawful and culpable, we must admit the extreme probability that we are heading for catastrophes even more terrible, even more uprooting, than those which many of us have witnessed during the last thirty-five years. For my part—and you must have realized this—not only do I not allow that it is possible for the philosopher to abstract from a situation which must unhesitatingly be qualified as eschato-logical, but I even deny his right to do so. Even if we need not subscribe to the idea—apocalyptic really—that we are already in the last period, the days that precede the end of the world and Christ's return, at least we have good grounds for a very serious belief that if this catastrophe comes to pass, it will mark the end of an historical era; and after that it is extremely difficult, almost impossible, to imagine what man's future can be.

Such being the case, it is perfectly legitimate for us to wonder what sort of help we can hope to find in the type of philo-sophy, some of the essential features of which I have tried to sketch in the course of these two series of lectures. Therein lies the fundamental question, and around it revolve the fol-lowing developments. I have often felt, it is true, that what I have tried to do is beyond my powers: but I should feel that I had completely failed in my purpose if I did not succeed in defining at least with a minimum of precision the spiritual attitude which we must adopt when we are faced by a situation which is indubitably without precedent in human history. It is of course quite absurd to try to comfort ourselves by imagining what might have been the horrors of the year 1000. Whatever may be said of them, those horrors were still in fact relatively infantile. Things are very different today; man has reached a point where not only does he regard himself as questionable (*fragwürdig*), or question his own being, but he works out methods of destruction, the use of which might well make the most densely populated parts of our planet un-inhabitable for an indefinite period; and this with the added horror that there is no possibility whatever of local-izing the effects. It is fruitless to put forward the objection that the range of these methods of destruction may be much smaller than we imagine; there is only one thing that matters, and that is the idea of them that is held, rightly or wrongly, by those who cold-bloodedly mean to use them during the awful struggle that has already begun. We are faced with the extension of totalitarianism to the cosmic, or at all events, the planetary, plane. Under such dreadful conditions, should we be right in saying that the considerations put forward in our discussion of faith or hope, may well be not only ineffective but also untimely? Ever since I realized that philosophy was my vocation, I have been at pains to keep clear of abstractions; and if we have managed to do so now, was it not by confining ourselves to the sphere of private experience? But is not this private experience, with all the treasures around which it is concentrated, itself threatened with destruction by the blind powers that have loosed themselves on the world?

But I must add another warning. Can we speak of blind powers in this connection, in the same way as we might be entitled to do if we were discussing an earthquake or a flood? While we must not be too hasty in saying that these powers are human in essence, we must at least confess that even if they are not 'of man', even if they are for example devilish, they have enlisted on their side instincts and passions which are indeed ours. It is actually extremely difficult, perhaps quite impossible for us to see what these powers are in themselves—even if we admit that these instincts or passions are only their vehicle, yet it is only *in them* and *through them* that they can be glimpsed. Moreover there are times when each one of us, provided he is quite sincere, can realize how open he is to contamination; and that is why he can pass on his own instincts or passions a judgment against which there is no appeal. His judgment has no bearing on something other than himself, which by its nature is a stranger to him; but he can speak unerringly of what he finds in the depths of his own self.

From another point of view, we must start by preventing ourselves from being intimidated by the gigantic as such, as were those primitive men who were much closer to us than we imagine. I should even go so far as to say that, spiritually speaking, everything which is gigantic is intrinsically suspect. It is probable that the most profound religions, Christianity in particular, have always felt this. There is no plane on which this is not true, and a young and very remarkable French sociologist, J. Bardet, is going to publish quite soon a work which I think of prime importance, in which he stresses the part which the increase in micro-mechanics can and must play in the humanization of industry. The same author condemns the sort of violence which man has done to nature during the last few centuries, and the ruinous consequences which have been its result for the economy of the human world. A superficial reader might think that such remarks had no metaphysical value, but in the perspective I have taken up during these lectures, it is obvious that they are of the utmost importance ; they apply to incarnate being, by which I mean the zone in which we have seen the conjunction of freedom and grace. Any sort of mechanical representation can only, indeed, distort the nature of this conjunction. We are in a position to become aware of it without being in any way able to understand how it happens; and it is here the part of secondary reflection to enable us to realize why this understanding is impossible —one might even go so far as to say, why this impossibility of understanding has a positive value, for we could not understand it without substituting for grace itself a natural power of a very dubious character. But when we see, for example, the waste of natural wealth of which in some places man has been guilty, we are at any rate prepared to condemn his unbridled misuse of gifts which have been granted him not by some external power which might be conceived by our imagination, but by Him whom we must call the Creator or the Father; gifts, to use a more metaphysical expression, whose source is the unrepresentable and uncharacterizable Being who constitutes us as existents.

It was not without design that I headed this last chapter by some concrete remarks which are mainly intended to draw your attention to the tragic issue which is at stake; their chief function in my mind, however, is to disclose the distinctive character of the propositions we have reached at the end of our enquiry.

The most important of these propositions consists, I think, in asserting philosophically, (that is to say short of any theological specification) the indissolubility of hope, of faith, and of charity. It is true that I have very seldom used the word 'charity' in my earlier lectures. But we cannot fail to see that intersubjectivity, which it is increasingly more evident is the cornerstone of a concrete ontology, is after all nothing but charity itself; I do not think I need decide whether it is a question of *agape* or *philia*—when the two notions, or the two ways of expressing it, are pushed sufficiently far they cannot but converge. As far as faith and hope, indeed, are concerned, one might be inclined at first to object by asking whether we have not known beings in whom faith seemed to be accompanied by a real deficiency in hope, perhaps even by a deep-rooted doubt of the spiritual import that can be attached to it. I think, however, that this apparent dissociation concerns only psychological consciousness. It may happen that my hope is vague or inarticulate to the point of seeming non-existent to me; but if I really have faith, this does not make the presence of hope in the depths of my being any less real, and I can doubt it only if the notion I form of hope is a constricting and distorting idea which amounts to confusing it with a personal desire for happiness. But, as I have explained, to hope cannot but be to hope for us—for all of us. It is an act which in some way embraces in itself the community which I constitute with all those who have been sharers of my own venture. Péguy, that great Frenchman who sang a clearer song of hope than any man of our own time, has many passages which might be quoted here. Another thing we should do is to look very closely at the type of universality with which we are here concerned. I should be prepared to say that it is essentially polyphonic, and that we shall be completely lost if we try to represent it to ourselves as in some way arithmetic, which is what is done by those who take as the starting point of their thought the mass or the multitude; that is to say the infra-individual and not the supra-personal. We can see how in our own time a most formidable confusion arises between those two spheres. There is still room for a more accurate determination of this point, but it is only in negative formulae that it can be done without distortion. We are in no position to know whether all human beings who now exist or who have existed are called or not to what we designate by a vague term, for which, however, there is no substitute—salvation. The truth goes further: these arithmetical operations can in the end apply only to things, to beings treated as things. In fact, however, the idea of salvation is empty of any meaning if it is referred to beings so treated.

At this point I may hazard a remark the significance of which must not be exaggerated; nor must it be taken as a dogmatic assertion: you have only to devote your attention for a short time to the hypothesis of successive reincarnations—an hypothesis which, in my opinion, the philosopher as such has no right whatever to dismiss as absurd—to realize that any arithmetical reckoning, wherever beings as such are concerned, is perhaps self-contradictory.

This may be an opportunity for stressing the fact that we must fight in ourselves without respite against that spirit of excommunication of which unhappily theologians, from whatever church they may claim their authority, have in the past afforded and sometimes still do afford, such distressing examples. The universality with which we are here concerned might be defined as a will for non-exclusion, and, which comes to the same thing, as a kind of spiritual welcoming, as opposed to all the ostracisms which derive from the spirit of abstraction.

This welcoming ought not of course to be identified with a spurious *syncretism*.

But here, as elsewhere, we have to take into account the fundamental fact that our condition is that of creatures, who can never cease to be such, and who are compelled to think of themselves only in this perspective. This amounts to saying that we are completely debarred from putting ourselves in the position of a judge who can pronounce exclusive judgments or even decide degrees of precedence. On the other hand it would be a serious mistake to interpret hope simply as an attitude that we have to take up: that would be as good as saying that we have to act as though we were hoping for all of us, the object of the hope being what one may call salvation—a word whose significance I shall shortly try to define more accurately. Here it is that faith comes in; it is the presence of faith that gives to hope its intelligible frame. This makes it all the more important to emphasize that we are always open to the temptation of interpreting faith itself in a purely voluntarist sense. It is precisely at this point that we can appreciate the full value of the line of thought we developed earlier concerning the bond between freedom and grace. Each one of us is in a position to recognize that his own essence is a *gift*—that it is not a *datum*; that he himself is a gift, and that he has no existence at all through himself. On the other hand, however, it is on the basis of that gift that freedom can grow or expand—that freedom which coincides with the trial in the course of which each man will have to make his own decision. This trial implies a decisive option. I can put my meaning to you by saying that the physical possibility of suicide which is engraved in our nature of incarnate beings is nothing but the expression of another much more profound and more hidden possibility, the possibility of a spiritual denial of self or, what comes to the same thing, of an impious and demoniac affirmation of self which amounts to a radical rejection of being. There is a sense in which that rejection is the final falsehood and absurdity; for it can exist only *through* someone who is; but as it becomes embodied it develops into perverted being.

It may perhaps be objected that if faith is understood in this sense, it does not seem to agree very closely with what is commonly meant by the word. The objector might ask me whether I have not systematically tried to shirk the fundamental question; that question will always be the existence of God. I am faced by two alternatives. Either I am in danger of reducing faith in God to an incommunicable psychic event, which implies the end of any sort of theology, and that means of all universality; or else I must try to find a way of framing something resembling a proof of the existence of God. The answer must be that everything we have said in the course of these lectures tends to show that this dilemma must be rejected—I should rather say transcended. It might well be that the idea of a proof, in the traditional sense of the word, of the existence of God, implied a paralogism or a vicious circle. To assess this correctly, it would be necessary to proceed to an analysis of the phenomenonological conditions of the act of proving. Proving always implies a 'I undertake to . . .' But this claim seems itself to be guaranteed not by the personal consciousness of a power, but by an essential unity which cannot but be apparent to a thought which has acquired for itself a certain degree of inner concentration. It is here that we can see the exemplary character of mathematical demonstration: whether or not it implies an intuition as its basis, is immaterial; for even if that intuition exists, it is something quite other than a subjective datum. One fact, however, remains: the proofs that have been given of the existence of God have not always seemed convincing—far from it—even to the historians of philosophy who expounded them the most minutely. We might say briefly that when they spoke of 'proofs' they put the word in inverted commas. We certainly cannot maintain that these historians failed to understand what they were saying. Should we, then, say that they had exposed a sophism which had escaped the notice of those who took the thought behind those proofs at its face value? That would be just as difficult to assert.

If the cosmological proof or the ontological proof 'mean nothing' to a man—which implies that as far as he can see they do not get their teeth into reality, they skate on its surface—it may be that he is no further advanced on the high road of thought than those who are satisfied by them (I have in mind, briefly, the fact that the Kantian argument set up in the Transcendental Dialectic does not seem to have finally exploded the proofs.) From another angle, however, I am no more inclined to think that those who wish to uphold the proofs can legitimately counter-attack by claiming that their opponents are guilty of a kind of fundamental ill-will which is basically pride. That is, indeed, too easy a method of discrediting one's opponent. In the first place this alleged ill-will calls for an effort of intelligent sympathy. We have reason to believe, as I have written before, that if the man against whom the charge is brought were to make his refusal fully explicit, he might say, 'I refuse to follow this road, because *it leads where I do not want to go*'. In one sense this is instructive, in another it is quite ambiguous. Why does the man not want to reach the affirmation of God which awaits him at the end of the journey? It may be because the affirmation seems to him incompatible with the fundamental data of experience, with the existence, for example, of suffering and all the forms which evil takes. A man like Albert Camus, for instance, cannot see how a God worthy of that name can tolerate the sufferings of children. But it may just as well be that in the atheist's eyes the affirmation of God would deaden the impulse that drives him, in his quality of free creature, to assert himself as an infinite in power; in that case, 'where I do not want to go' would mean 'I do not want God to be, because He cannot be without limiting me, that is, denying me'. This explains the singular fact that what the 'prover' puts forward as perfection is taken in an entirely opposite sense by

his opponent; the latter takes it as an obstacle to the expansion
of his own more or less divinized being, as a negation, that is,
of the Sovereign Good. What is lacking here is the necessary
minimum of agreement about ends, about the supreme value.
But every proof presupposes, if it is to be given, at least this
minimum of agreement. When that is lacking, the conditions
in which proof is even possible are no longer present. The history of modern philosophy, as I said before, seems to supply
abundant illustrations of the progressive replacement of
atheism, in the grammatically privative sense of the word, by
an anti-theism whose mainspring is the will that God should not
be. If, then, we consider the ineffectual character of the
proofs of the existence of God, we cannot but notice again
that deep split in the world of men to which I called your
attention at the beginning of last year's lectures. So we stumble
on this paradox: the proofs are ineffectual precisely when they
would be most necessary, when, that is, it is a question of
convincing an unbeliever; conversely, when belief is already
present and when, accordingly, there is the minimum of
agreement, then they seem to serve no useful purpose. If a
man has experienced the presence of God, not only has he no
need of proofs, he may even go so far as to consider the idea
of a demonstration as a slur on what is for him a sacred evidence.
Now, from the point of view of a philosophy of existence,
it is this sort of testimony which is the central and irreducible
datum. When, on the other hand, the presence of God is no
longer—I shall not say felt, but recognized, then there is
nothing which is not questionable, and when man models
himself on Lucifer, that questioning degenerates into the negative will which I have already described. Can I hope to show
this Lucifer-man his mistake? The truth seems to be that there

is room for only one thing here, and that is a conversion which no creature can flatter himself he is capable of bringing about. There is hardly any phrase which is more detestable than 'so and so has *made* so many conversions'. It amounts to dragging conversion to the level of a piece of magic. Spiritually speaking such a comparison is outrageous. This, we have seen, is the domain of grace; it is also the domain of intersubjectivity, where all causal interpretations are a mistake.

All this is an illustration of the essentially paradoxical situation, in Kierkegaard's sense of the word, we find ourselves in when we are in the presence of God. Nothing we have said here can enable us to minimize its distressful and agonizing character; and yet it should by now be manifest that from the point of view I have adopted, anguish is not and cannot be the last word. I should be so bold as to say, on the contrary, that the last word must be with love and joy; and this I say from my innermost heart. If we want to satisfy ourselves of the truth of this, we must emphasize the intelligible aspect of faith; and in doing so, we shall be obliged to diverge very considerably from the views both of the Danish philosopher and even perhaps of the writer in whom we may well be inclined to see his precursor—I mean Pascal; for there is a connection which it is the philosopher's duty to underline with the utmost emphasis, the connection which binds together faith and the spirit of truth. Whenever a gap begins to open between these two, it is a proof either that faith is tending to degenerate into idolatry or else that the spirit of truth is becoming arid and giving way to ratiocinative reason; and I think we have made it amply clear that this split is contrary to its nature, to its own proper impulse. The spirit of truth is nothing if it is not a light which is seeking for the light; intelligibility is nothing if it is not at once a coming together and the nuptial joy which is inseparable from this coming together. The more I tend to raise myself towards this Uncreated Light, without which I am left in the dark—which would mean that I have no being at all—the more I in some way advance in faith. Alternatively one might say that therein is to be found one possible way of progress at least, and it is the one which it is certainly the philosopher's duty to mark out first. If it is looked at in this way, the voluntarist error is seen in all its gravity, in as much at least as will is distinct from intelligence—a distinction, however, whose value is really quite superficial. A will without intelligence would be a mere impulse, and an intelligence which lacked will would be devitalized. But we shall only make it possible for ourselves, I shall not say to understand faith, but to discover some of its essential characteristics, if we establish ourselves at the ideal point of junction of these wrongly dissociated faculties; and we could, of course, add to this analogous statements concerning affectivity in its relations with intelligence and will. One can never keep too clearly in mind that the act of faith, the '*I believe*', is the act of the person considered in his concrete unity; that does not mean, however, except in the case of the saint, that around this act there is not bound to be a fringe of hesitation or even of unspoken refusal. It is in the light of these reflections that we should look at the question of knowing whether our belief is to be our own responsibility. Here again, I think, we must take a *via media*. To say that the act of faith is a free act is to put it ambiguously; it is true only if we take up the line we did before when we were speaking of freedom. The truth is that we have to rid ourselves of prejudices which block the path to faith, or again to make ourselves open to grace—although that does not imply that grace is automatically released for us; and we can see that the more clearly when we realize that it is not comparable to a force. There is no doubt, however, but that we must add that this reflection which thus operates in a way before grace, certainly implies in its origin something which is of the same order as grace. 'Everything', says Bernanos' country priest, 'is grace.'* But that saying is one that can be uttered with complete sincerity only by a saint. Were I, for example, to say it, I could not do so without reservations which would make it only a half-truth; for we must insist again that here we are in the existential; a word (*une parole*) as such cannot be reduced to a content which is to be assessed according to pre-existing standards: there is a being for whom it is 'my word'; it is supported, very unequally supported moreover, by the man who utters it. I can, it is true, say that the saint is right, but if I am fully assured that he is I shall certainly have to follow him on the road of sanctity. Here again we have the fundamental idea of an existential weight in the assertion; but it cannot be understood if we cling to a monadist conception. It is only on the plane of intersubjectivity that certain contradictions or semi-contradictions can survive; they must, moreover, develop one way or the other; either they become more pronounced, or they have the contrary tendency to be resolved, finally to disappear, but this can take place only, I think, in a world which is no longer ours and which is beyond the compass of our imagination. I can believe in another man's faith without that faith becoming absolutely my own; but if I make myself at home in that position, there is a danger that it may become a lie. If, on the other hand, I strive to release myself from that attitude without being com-

*In *Le Journal d'un Curé de Campagne*.

pletely successful in doing so, then it will be found that it can help me on the road to salvation.

Once again our thoughtful attention is drawn to this word 'salvation'. Can we define its philosophical significance more exactly, without encroaching on the strictly theological sphere? The first question to answer would be under what conditions the idea can hold a meaning for us. For a start, I think, evil must be recognized as presenting a certain reality, I might almost say a certain substance. That was my meaning in suggesting its identity with death. Salvation is nothing if it does not deliver us from death. But the connection with what we said about hope is quite clear enough for us to be justified in stating the principle that all hope is a hope of salvation. But can this final deliverance be thought of, say, in the temporal universe such as we see it, the universe in which we are caught up in our quality of terrestrial beings? The great illusion which seems to be the solace of the followers of Marx or even of Hegel, appears to me to lie in that belief. The truth is rather that there is not and cannot be any salvation in a world whose very structure makes it liable to death. Are we to imagine some perfection of technique which would alter this actual structure? That, I fear, is quite fictitious. If we really look deeply into the matter, we shall be obliged to ask whether death is not in some way the price to be paid for sin, though we should not take that literally nor apply it within the framework of individual existence. If that is true, it is inconceivable that technique—and it does not matter what form it may take—can ever overcome death. At the same time, I am far from blind to the difficulties involved in this notion, the notion, I mean, that we can form of sin; but I cannot at this point think of undertaking a full statement on this matter.

We are again in the order of what can be found and taken into account rather than of what can be understood. My meaning, however, is in no way that every man is necessarily conscious of having himself sinned. It may well be that even while he accuses himself of the faults of which any man has been guilty in the course of his life, he still maintains that he entirely lacks this feeling. But if he is in good faith, he will have at least to admit that he is much too closely bound to those who are manifestly sinners to be able to protest his innocence like the Pharisees. 'There is a communion of sinners', says one of my characters. Each one of us is involved at all events in countless structures in which a spirit of good faith cannot fail to perceive the presence of sin.

This may be too much for your patience, and you will ask what definition of sin can be suggested? What we can say, I think, is that all authentic sin is sin against the light; in other words, against the universal. At root, it is the act of shutting oneself in on oneself or of taking one's own self as the centre. On this point, moreover, all the great religions seem to be in agreement. Again, however, it is not only a question of individual acts, but of something which has the appearance of a world or a kingdom; or, better, of an anti-kingdom. We must not, then, follow the catechism class and say that death is the wages of sin. Its implications are infinitely more complex and obscure. Let it be enough for us to acknowledge that the world of sin is a world in which death is in some way *at home*. That slight phrase is the most precise expression we can give to the connection which we must trace. On the other hand we cannot fail to see with equal clarity that if this world can be conquered, it can only be in the thick of a hard and even tragic fight; in this fight we have to engage in conditions which are not of our choosing, neither are they strictly speaking imposed from without; in reality they form a part of our vocation. The extreme difficulty which we confront in such a matter arises from the fact that we cannot do without the assistance of imagery; or we can put it more accurately by saying that if we try to dispense with imagery, there is a danger of relapsing into abstraction. The relation between the philosopher and the man of religion which has to be established here is probably not that which Spinoza, for example, conceived; for Spinoza almost certainly under-estimated the value of imagination as a concrete and positive stimulative power. Must not the philosopher admit that we cannot really free ourselves from some key-images—for example that of heaven as the abode of the blessed—provided that he shows that these images are bound up with the conditions of existence which belong to a wayfaring creature, and that they cannot accordingly be considered as literally true. In this sense I would say, for example, that heaven can hardly appear to us, who are of the earth, as other than the sky above; but in so far as the bond which holds us to the earth is relaxed or changes its nature, it will be bound to present a different aspect to us. We are fated to undergo a metamorphosis whose nature we can foresee only very imperfectly, and it is just on the idea of this metamorphosis that rests the revival of orphism whose imperious demands must be familiar to many of us today. Hence again it follows that salvation can also be better conceived by us as a road rather than a state; and this links up again with some profound views of the Greek Fathers, in particular St. Gregory of Nyssa.

I may add that if there is a sense in which salvation is indistinguishable from peace, it is a living peace that is in question;

it is certainly not a spiritual stand-still, our being as such getting congealed in the contemplation of some fixed star. This living peace, however, could be nothing but a progress in love and in truth, the consolidation, that is, of an intelligible city which is at the same time and above all else a city of souls. From this point of view, it is perhaps on the Christian idea of the mystical body that the philosopher may be called to concentrate his attention.

From this we may see, as we have long been able to anticipate, that every philosophy which is still to any extent in the grip of history and historical categories, thereby betrays the exigence of transcendence which has been the connecting thread of all our enquiry. If such a conception is condemned on the ground that it does not conform to the sense of history, then that condemnation cannot be taken as acceptable. We are in a position to discern that this notion of the sense of history is itself full of ambiguity and will probably break down under analysis. It may well be that we are witnessing a deterioration of the human species and of the existential modalities that have characterized it in what are called civilized periods. This can be contested only if one endorses the eighteenth-century optimism, of which Marx, when all is said and done, is still the heir, and accepts as a principle that the movement of history can be only towards a sort of fulfilment. But if that assertion is stripped of all strictly religious reference, it becomes no more than a completely arbitrary postulate. The simple fact that we have been able to witness the re-establishment of slavery, and that on a colossal scale, the re-introduction, that is, of a state of affairs which men who lived at the end of the nineteenth century believed to be overthrown for ever, is sufficient to arouse the gravest doubts. I realize, of course, that if the reality of progress is affirmed *on religious grounds*, it puts the matter in a very different light. But, unless we are bound to subscribe to an essentially rationalist deism, we must admit that we cannot see what lies behind God's plans; we cannot force them into rational frames like those in which a man confines himself who speculates ingenuously on the beneficial consequences which the progress of science entails for mankind, provided that it has at last become conscious of its mistakes and crimes. It is precisely on the awakening of this consciousness, that our doubts must bear. What right have we to suppose that the disasters it has suffered will eventually open the eyes of the mass of humanity? The ghastly experience of more than thirty years leaves little room for optimism on this point; and, granted that the survivors of a new war may be able to draw some elementary lesson from it, we may feel doubtful about the spiritual quality of this incipient wisdom. As we have already seen, everything goes to show that the alternative lies between conversion and non-conversion; our final task must be to attempt an elucidation of the meaning of this conversion.

In the first place, let us make no attempt to hide our ignorance. We cannot even get an inkling of the conditions under which such conversions can take place, for, by definition, they lie beyond the power of our own incentive. It may be that they are of the specifically miraculous order. I do not see that the philosopher has any right to exclude such a possibility. I would even say that they are almost certainly of the miraculous order, without implying either that the miracle in question is of the physical order or that grace necessarily manifests itself through materially super-normal phenomena. What is more important and more within our powers, is to see in what this conversion can consist. Can it affect the will exclusively? That, however, would be to reinstate the distinction I have already rejected. Change of will cannot itself automatically be bound up with the change in the light thrown upon life, and I wonder whether in the last analysis it is not with a supra-temporalization of the latter that we have to deal. This is a most difficult matter, and I shall try to be as explicit as it permits.

The first thing is to avoid a possible misunderstanding: it cannot be a question, strictly speaking, of our overstepping the bounds of time; that would be an escape into pure abstraction. What we have to do, I think, is rather to get rid of a certain temporal schematization, which in reality is applicable only to things and to ourselves only in so far as we can be assimilated to things. Unhappily the world of men is becoming more and more organized as though such an assimilation could be completely effected to the last detail; such, it seems, is the state of affairs to which the applied sciences are directed when they are in the service of a totalitarian state which is progressively more radically technocratic. In *Le Monde des Accusés*, for example, a recent book by the young German novelist Walter Jens, or in George Orwell's *Nineteen Eighty-four*, that situation is described with realistic and terrifying accuracy. We may note, however, that in this situation terror still plays a leading part; but we can, if necessary, imagine a mechanization of human relations so ruthless that there would be no need to rely on terror, which may be required only during a period of transition.

Still, a reflection which is kept alive by contemplation discloses this, that our world is integrally doomed to destruction,

and this for the profound reason that it is already itself destruction. It is just such a world to which we have to refuse
our assent, even if it enrols us by force, even if it tries to
crush us and goes so far as to do so physically. We must
maintain that in so far as we are not things, in so far as we
refuse to allow ourselves to be reduced to the condition of
things, we belong to an entirely different world-dimension,
and it is this dimension which can and must be called supra-
temporal. 'One thing I found after the death of my parents',
says one of the principal characters in a recent play of mine*
'It was that what we call survival is really *undervival*; we
find that those whom we have never ceased to love with all
that is best in us, become a sort of throbbing vault: it is invisible, but yet we can just feel its presence, it almost touches us;
as we move forward under it we have to bend ourselves
lower and lower; we become more and more drawn out
of our own selves until the moment when everything has
been swallowed up in love.' We should, I think, devote much
thought to this profession of faith of Antoine Sorgue in
L'Émissaire; to Arnaud Chartrain's phrase, too, in *La Soif*, 'In
death we shall lay ourselves open to what we have lived on when
we were on earth'. In other words we must become aware
that we are literally arched over by a living reality; it is
certainly incomparably more alive than our own, and we
belong to it to the extent, unhappily a very limited extent,
to which we release ourselves from the schematizations to
which I have referred. The great service that philosophy
should render us—and here, of course, I fall in line with one
of the great Platonic themes—would be constantly to increase
our awareness, even this side of death, of this reality which
quite certainly surrounds us on all sides, but from which,

* *L'Emissaire*, Paris, 1949

thanks to our condition of free beings, we have the awful power systematically to withhold ourselves. Everything goes to show with increasing clarity that the power is given to us of in some way locking ourselves more firmly in the prison in which we elect to live. That is the terrible price we have to pay for the incomprehensible power we have been given, or which, still more, makes us to be 'ourselves'. On the other hand, in so far as we allow ourselves to give ear to the solicitations—countless in number even if slight in substance—which come to us from the invisible world, then the whole outlook undergoes a change: and by that I mean that the transformation takes place *here below*, for earthly life itself is at the same time transfigured, it clothes itself in a dignity which cannot be allowed to it if it is looked at as some sort of excrescence which has budded erratically on a world which is in itself foreign to the spirit and to all its demands. Let me make use again of one of the musical comparisons for which you know I have a taste, and say that from the moment when we open ourselves to these infiltrations of the invisible, we cease to be the unskilled and yet pretentious soloists we perhaps were at the start, and gradually become members, wide-eyed and brotherly, of an orchestra in which those whom we so inaptly call the dead are quite certainly much closer to Him of whom we should not perhaps say that He conducts the symphony, but that He *is* the symphony in its profound and intelligible unity; a unity in which we can hope to be included only by degrees, through individual trials, the sum total of which, though it cannot be foreseen by each of us, is inseparable from his own vocation.

I agree that all I have said does not reach as far as revelation, properly so called, and dogma. But it is at least a way of approaching it; it is a difficult road and strewn with obstacles, but it is by following this pilgrim road that we can hope one day to see the radiance of that eternal Light of which a reflection has continually shone on us all the time we have been in this world—that Light without whose guidance we may be sure that we should never have started our journey.